SpringerBriefs in Criminology

SpringerBriefs in Criminology present concise summaries of cutting edge research across the fields of Criminology and Criminal Justice. It publishes small but impactful volumes of between 50-125 pages, with a clearly defined focus. The series covers a broad range of Criminology research from experimental design and methods, to brief reports and regional studies, to policy-related applications.

The scope of the series spans the whole field of Criminology and Criminal Justice, with an aim to be on the leading edge and continue to advance research. The series will be international and cross-disciplinary, including a broad array of topics, including juvenile delinquency, policing, crime prevention, terrorism research, crime and place, quantitative methods, experimental research in criminology, research design and analysis, forensic science, crime prevention, victimology, criminal justice systems, psychology of law, and explanations for criminal behavior.

SpringerBriefs in Criminology will be of interest to a broad range of researchers and practitioners working in Criminology and Criminal Justice Research and in related academic fields such as Sociology, Psychology, Public Health, Economics and Political Science.

More information about this series at http://www.springer.com/series/10159

Chelsea A. Binns • Robin J. Kempf

Safety and Security in Hotels and Home Sharing

Springer

Chelsea A. Binns
Security, Fire, and Emergency Management
John Jay College of Criminal Justice
New York, NY, USA

Robin J. Kempf
School of Public Affairs
University of Colorado Colorado Springs
Colorado Springs, CO, USA

ISSN 2192-8533 ISSN 2192-8541 (electronic)
SpringerBriefs in Criminology
ISBN 978-3-030-59305-6 ISBN 978-3-030-59306-3 (eBook)
https://doi.org/10.1007/978-3-030-59306-3

This Springer imprint is published by the registered company Springer Nature Switzerland AG
The registered company address is: Gewerbestrasse 11, 6330 Cham, Switzerland

This brief is dedicated to our daughters, Samantha and Alison, to whom we wish all the safety and security in their travels throughout the world.

Preface

Home sharing, or opening your house for strangers to stay, for a fee, has expanded so fast that public policy has not been able to keep up. This book explores the implications of the different treatment in the United States of hotels versus home sharing for safety and security. Specifically, hotels are heavily regulated for the protection of hotel guests, employees, and property, whereas home sharing in the United States is almost completely unregulated. These disparate regulatory schemes have important impacts on the safety and security of property and persons in home sharing, of which the general public likely is unaware. The policy issues are in need of a close examination. This brief should help in that task by placing safety and security concerns in hotels versus home sharing side by side.

Chapter 1 provides an overview of the work's central thesis and research questions. Chapter 2 presents background on the hospitality industry broadly. Chapter 3 examines existing crime and safety data relevant to home sharing. Chapter 4 explores the laws and regulations that apply to hotels versus home sharing. Chapter 5 compares and contrasts the contemporary safety and security practices in both settings. Chapter 6 delves into the relevant criminological theories related to safety and security when sleeping away from home. Chapter 7 briefly examines the impact of COVID-19 on the topic at hand. Finally, Chap. 8 presents conclusions and policy recommendations concerning safety and security in home sharing.

The authors wish to acknowledge the hard work and contributions of our research assistants, Shea Hastings Connors, Julien Roussell, and Benjamin Defibaugh. Thanks also to Peter Haxton for his editing help and to Asher Fergusson for his consultation. This work was supported by funding from Our Neighborhoods.

New York, NY, USA — Chelsea A. Binns
Colorado Springs, CO, USA — Robin J. Kempf

Contents

1 Introduction to Safety and Security in Hotels and Home Sharing 1
1.1 Definitions 3
What 3
Who 3
Where 4
1.2 Central Thesis and Research Questions 4
Works Cited 7

2 What Is Home Sharing in Relation to the Hospitality Industry? 11
2.1 The Commercial Landscape of Hospitality 11
2.2 Conclusion 13
Works Cited 14

3 What Do We Learn from the Crime and Safety Data on Home Shares? 15
3.1 Security Concerns in Hotels and Home Shares 17
Unique Crimes in the Home-Sharing Setting 17
3.2 Safety Concerns in Hotels and Home Shares 23
3.3 Conclusion 23
Works Cited 24

4 Who Has Legal Responsibility for Safety and Security in Hotels Versus Home Sharing? 29
4.1 Other Legal and Regulatory Responsibilities Placed on Hotels 31
4.2 A Hotel's Protections from Guests' Behavior 32
4.3 Laws on Safety and Security in Home Shares 33
4.4 Local Attempts to Regulate Home Sharing 35
4.5 What Legal Options Are Available to Guests and Hosts to Do If They Are Wronged in a Home-Sharing Situation? 39
4.6 Conclusion 40
Works Cited 40

5 What Are the Contemporary Safety and Security Practices Used in Hotels and Home Shares? ... 43
5.1 Safety and Security Concerns and Measures Taken to Address Them ... 44
5.2 What Guidance Does Airbnb Provide to Its Users Regarding Safety and Security? ... 44
5.3 Based on Contemporary Practices, How Does a Guest Decide Whether to Stay in a Hotel or a Home Share? ... 52
5.4 Conclusion ... 56
Works Cited ... 56

6 What Does Criminological Theory Suggest About Sleeping Away from Home? ... 59
6.1 Defensible Space Theory Suggests Buildings and Homes Can Be Designed to Be More Secure, But Residents Must Play a Role in Providing Security ... 59
6.2 Rational Choice Theory Suggests Hotel and Home-Sharing Crime Can Be Prevented by Reducing Opportunities for Crime and Increasing Punishment for Bad Acts ... 65
6.3 Routine Activity Theory Suggests That Guests of Both Hotels and Home Shares Can Thwart Crime ... 68
6.4 Conclusion ... 71
Works Cited ... 72

7 What Issues About Home Sharing Has the Advent of COVID-19 Exposed? ... 77
7.1 Conclusion ... 80
Works Cited ... 80

8 Conclusions, Policy Recommendations, Limitations, and Suggestions for Future Research ... 83
8.1 Policy Recommendations ... 86
8.2 Limitations and Future Research ... 88
8.3 Conclusion ... 88
Works Cited ... 89

Works Cited ... 91

Index ... 95

Chapter 1
Introduction to Safety and Security in Hotels and Home Sharing

Travel and tourism services are important to the world's economy. In 2019, prior to the advent of COVID-19, these services generated $8.9 trillion, accounting for 10.3% of the global gross domestic product (GDP) (World Travel and Tourism Council 2020). Hotels, on one hand, and home-sharing providers, on the other, are key contributors to travel and tourism, providing places for guests to sleep when away from home. Hotels are in the full-time business of hospitality, whereas home-sharing companies connect property owners or renters with individuals looking for a place to stay for the short term, providing an alternative to hotels. Yet they are not the same when it comes to their legal classification, regulatory environment, and safety and security features, the focus of this brief.

To compare, US hotels include nearly 55,900 properties with 5.3 million guestrooms that sell almost 1.3 billion rooms annually (Oxford Economics 2019). In 2018, hotels supported $659.4 billion of the United States's gross domestic product (Oxford Economics 2019). Hotel operations and guest spending supported 8.3 million jobs and $395 billion in total labor income (Oxford Economics 2019).

A relative newcomer to the hospitality scene, Airbnb, the largest home-sharing company,[1] touts 500,000 listings in the United States, with 11% reserved each night (MuchNeeded.com 2020). (Worldwide, it offered more than 7 million listings in 2019, with over 2 million people staying in an Airbnb on a given night (Airbnb n.d.-b)). Even with its comparatively small size, Airbnb, a private company, has been identified as a top industry "disruptor" for innovating and revolutionizing the industry (CNBC.com Staff 2019). In 2019, Airbnb reported a direct contribution to the US economy of $34 billion[2] (Airbnb 2019). In New York City, Airbnb calculated its

[1] For this reason, Airbnb will frequently be used as the primary example of home-sharing companies throughout this report.

[2] This figure is based on the sum of hosts' earnings and an estimate of guests' expenditures while traveling.

C. A. Binns, R. J. Kempf, *Safety and Security in Hotels and Home Sharing*, SpringerBriefs in Criminology, https://doi.org/10.1007/978-3-030-59306-3_1

presence supported 4500 jobs and generated $632 million in economic activity in 2013 (Airbnb 2013). Airbnb's economic impact studies in other primary markets such as San Francisco, Paris, Berlin, Amsterdam, London, Edinburgh, Sydney, and Barcelona have also reported positive economic impact in the form of local spending, jobs, and income for local host households (Airbnb 2019).

Home-sharing companies, such as Airbnb and VRBO, are able to compete with hotels by offering a large selection of homely settings at lower prices. A 2016 study found the average daily rate for an Airbnb rental was $160.47 whereas a hotel room was $163.90 (Griswold 2016). Studies have shown consumers can rent a house in the United States on Airbnb for the same price as a hotel room (Griswold 2016). Further, Airbnb offers more rooms in some geographic areas than some of the largest hotel chains (Mudallal 2015). In 2014, Airbnb offered 1 million rooms in Europe while InterContinental Hotels Group (IHG), the largest hotel company in Europe,[3] offered about 698,000 rooms.

This competition has caused people to book fewer hotel rooms. A 2018 study showed that in the US cities with the largest Airbnb market share, Airbnb results in 1.3% fewer hotel nights booked and a 1.5% loss in hotel revenue (Farronato and Fradkin 2018; Gerdeman 2018). While Airbnb doesn't generate the same revenue as hotels, this "disruption" is a cause of concern for hotels as guests look elsewhere to stay.

Yet, what guests may not be fully aware of is that regardless of similarities in service provided, these two competitive hospitality sectors are subject to completely different sets of laws and regulations, especially when it comes to the safety and security of those involved. One reason for this policy variation is the fact that home-sharing companies own no real estate, and thus, appear to have a different legal status than companies such as Marriott International or Wyndham Worldwide. Another reason is that the Federal Communications Commission has taken the position that Internet platforms connecting service providers with users like Airbnb and VRBO, as well as eBay, Uber, and Etsy, are shielded from all liability arising from the behavior of users of their platforms. Further, while hotels are subject to a plethora of laws and regulations, home sharing is not. Although local jurisdiction like New York City, Miami, and San Francisco are trying to take steps to regulate home sharing, no one is legally tasked with protecting safety and security in the home-sharing arena. This is true even though home sharing gives rise to unique crime-related concerns on the part of both home-sharing hosts and guests.

This brief explores issues of safety and security in the home-sharing setting as they compare to those of hotels. But first, key terms relevant to this exploration must be defined.

[3] Size here is measured by the number of rooms.

1.1 Definitions

What

Safety Concerns In this brief, safety concerns are those issues that an individual might worry about when sleeping away from home that occurs unintentionally or by accident. These issues, from a fire to a slip-and-fall, may be caused by human carelessness, inattentiveness, lack of training, or other unintentional events (Fennelly 2016).

Safety Measures Safety measures are those approaches, including people, procedures, or equipment, that are taken to prevent or detect abnormal conditions that can unintentionally endanger people, property, or the enterprise.

Security Concerns Although scholars have noted the challenge when it comes to defining security (Brooks 2010), in this brief, security concerns are those issues that an individual might worry about when sleeping away from home that are a result of intentional, malevolent human actions. These may include theft, vandalism, physical violence, terrorism, or other intentional attacks (Fennelly 2016).

Security Measures Security measures include those approaches, including people, procedures, or equipment, that are taken to protect people, property, or the enterprise from intentional malevolent human threats.

Who

Hotels For purposes of the present research, the term "hotel" generically refers to an enterprise with the primary business to provide lodging to the public. This lodging may include meals, entertainment, or personal services. As used here, "hotel" includes hotels, motels, inns, bed and breakfasts (BandBs), and other similar types of businesses. The biggest providers in this space are Marriott International, Wyndham Worldwide Corporation, Hilton Worldwide Holdings, Choice Hotels International, and InterContinental Hotel Group.

Home-Sharing Companies This term refers to those companies that have established Internet-based platforms or websites that connect people who wish to welcome strangers to stay temporarily in their homes, or portions of their homes, for a fee. The most well-known providers in this space are Airbnb, VRBO, and HomeAway, the latter two being owned by the same company.

Hosts In this study, the term "hosts" refers generally to individuals sharing their homes and/or apartments with others through Internet platforms for a fee (Marzen et al. 2017). These property owners are not in the primary business of providing lodging to the public. Hosts might be offering their entire space for rent while they are not on the premises, or they might be "sharing" their dwelling with a guest, who has rented one of their rooms. A host might be offering a single property on a home-sharing platform or hundreds of properties – or anything in between.

It is important to note that hosts can vary in terms of their particular legal/ownership situation. Hosts might be the legal owners of a property via deed or mortgage. The host could also be a legal renter of a property, who is subletting their space, legally or illegally (depending on the landlord's lease) through home sharing. In rare occasions, the host could also be a sub-subletter, i.e., a sublessee who is now subletting the property.[4]

Guests This term refers to individuals who pay for temporary lodging in either a hotel or home-sharing setting.

Users of Home Sharing This term refers to both guests and hosts who are connected through the platform of a home-sharing company.

Where

Even though both hotels and home sharing are found globally, the laws and regulations discussed in this work, as well as the implications thereof, are limited to the United States.

1.2 Central Thesis and Research Questions

The central thesis of this work focuses on the responsibility for safety and security in hotels and home-sharing services.[5] The aim of this research is to determine who is responsible for guest safety and security in each setting as well as the type of security typically provided under each model. Thus, this brief comparatively reviews the security and safety features of hotels and home-sharing services. It analyzes the applicable crime data, laws, and theories to determine responsibility for crime control and prevention in both sectors. Ultimately, this research shows that *the responsibility that is largely placed on the hotel shifts to the home-sharing hosts and guests, while the home-sharing company that sets up the transaction has no responsibility at all.* This is a counterintuitive result, and as such, it is the goal of this brief

[4]This situation is rarely legal, but it's possible it was "permitted" due to an oversight of an individual lease's terms, etc.

[5]Safety and security is defined here as protecting persons and property from unintentional and intentional harm, respectively.

to provide readers with the information necessary to improve their personal safety and security when using home-sharing services.

This work is timely and important. As the use of home sharing has proliferated, so have safety and security concerns. Major headlines have appeared throughout the world reporting crimes and accidents occurring in home-sharing settings – many of which are unique to home sharing. These give rise to questions of the apportionment of responsibility in these situations.

Further, a full examination of the challenges of addressing safety and security in home-sharing settings as compared to hotels is overdue. Previous scholarly works have explored crime and security in hotels (Hua and Yang 2017; Feickert et al. 2006; Groenenboom and Jones 2003; Gill et al. 2002; Lisante 1972). Others have explored home sharing generally, including a review of new local regulatory schemes (Palombo 2015; McNamara 2015). Still others examine how to generally control crime, and prevent accidents but do not examine hotel or home-sharing settings (see, e.g., Enz 2009; Herbert 1999; Gottfredson and Hirschi 1995; Braithwaite 1982). This brief brings these three elements together: the legal landscape that applies to hotels and home sharing; the unique safety and security practices and features of hotels as compared to home sharing; and theories on accident and crime control and prevention. From this, a clearer picture of the roles and responsibilities of individuals in home-sharing settings emerges.

Hotel safety and security practices offer a strong baseline to compare the home-sharing model against. Hotels still experience incidents, but many types of safety issues and crimes are less likely due to their preventative actions. Hotels generally have very robust safety and security programs and procedures, only some of which they are legally obligated to provide. Comparing the typical hotel practices to those found – or not found – in home sharing serves to increase the users' general understanding of vulnerabilities in both industries. The differences in their security postures are expected to be reflected in the outcomes the entities pursue. Since these outcomes have not been analyzed to date, the information presented here will be new data. This comparison highlights the implications of making users of home-sharing services (both guests and hosts) reliant on themselves to protect their own safety and provide their own security.

This research explores the following six primary questions:

- What is home sharing in relation to the hospitality industry?
- What do we learn from the safety and crime data on home shares?
- Who has legal responsibility for safety and security in hotels versus home sharing?
- What are contemporary safety and security practices used in hotels and home shares?
- What does criminological theory suggest about sleeping away from home?
- What issues about home sharing has the advent of COVID-19 exposed?

In answering these questions, important findings in terms of crime typologies and security outcomes (or objectives) are presented. First, while crime inevitably occurs in both settings, the types of crimes vary due to the difference in security models. For instance, in the regulated hotel setting, fewer victims are expected, in part because the "hosts" are licensed corporate entities and not members of the general public, whereas the absence of security-related regulations in the home-sharing service sector has helped foster in the emergence of a unique set of crimes affecting both hosts and guests.

Second, in terms of security outcomes, there are important differences between these industries. Although users of any service are always expected to take personal security precautions, guests of hotels may assume certain levels of security are present and be less protective of themselves on a personal level. The absence of formal security in the home-sharing environment leads to confusion about the provision of security protections. Who is responsible if no one is? Further complicating matters is the absence of expertise on the part of home-sharing users. Many users of these services may lack awareness of their security responsibilities as well as the ability to provide it.

It is the goal of this work to illuminate who is responsible for an individual's safety and security in the home-sharing sector and help control crime by doing the following:

- Examining relevant safety and crime data to identify the types of crimes committed in hotels versus the home-sharing setting
- Setting forth the laws and regulations related to safety and security in both settings, including the attempts of New York City to regulate home sharing
- Analyzing the applicable scholarly theories on crime control, including rational choice, routine activity, and defensible space theories
- Making suggestions about safety and security that could benefit users of home sharing

That the responsibility for safety and security shifts from hotels to home-sharing hosts and guests is a policy decision with crucial tradeoffs that can have dire consequences. It is thought that the shift in accountability for one's safety and security from the traditional responsibility allocation is not widely understood. Thus, despite some efforts by companies like Airbnb, for example, to educate its users, it is likely that many guests and hosts do not realize they have said responsibility until something bad happens. In fact, the general public should be especially vigilant when home sharing. While home sharing may cost less, this cost savings is due in part to reduced safety and security services that must be supplemented by the user.

Both home-sharing hosts and guests are at risk. Hosts risk damages to and theft of their property, because basic safety and security processes are not mandated, and therefore, not performed. For example, a typical security process employed by hotels is to verify guests' identification. Hotels also permit users to book rooms under assumed names for privacy reasons (Magalhães et al. 2017). However, hotels require identification from all guests in person when completing their booking. Hotels are also commercial operations with security personnel on hand. If there are any issues with a guest, someone will be able to assist.

It is a very different situation for a private home owner. According to an online forum for Airbnb hosts, guests are known to book home shares under assumed names.[6] Even though Airbnb states they verify users' identities, by comparing names to an officially issued form of identification, there is no way for the company to know whether the ID and the guest represent the same person. This means that a host may not know the true identity of their guest until the person is already on their property. This presents a security concern; however, hosts may not realize this is a problem unless a guest does something bad.

On the other hand, guests risk life and limb to safety and security problems. An example is the installation of smoke or carbon monoxide detectors. Hotels are mandated to do so, which is confirmed by inspection. Airbnb does not require hosts to obtain these devices, and they do not conduct safety inspections on their listed properties.[7] Airbnb states on its website that they will provide these detectors for free to hosts who ask for them; however, detectors are optional. In the safety section of their website, Airbnb advises guests to look for the notice of smoke detectors and carbon monoxide detectors in their hosts' listings; however, the truth of the presence of such detectors can only be ascertained after the guest has physically arrived at the host's property. This represents an important safety issue. Airbnb also advises guests to bring their own carbon monoxide detector on their vacation, but do most guests actually do this? It is more likely that guests don't realize they should have brought one until it is too late.

There are also negative spillover effects to neighborhoods where home sharing occurs in regard to the entire community's safety and security. Thus, neighbors have a vested interest in how home sharing occurs in their localities.

Ultimately, this work concludes that safety and security in home sharing is a crucial issue that deserves more attention from both users and policymakers. This brief serves to educate home-sharing users, both guests and hosts, about their role in ensuring their own safety and security, which is starkly different from what is taken for granted in a hotel setting. Further, this brief helps policymakers better understand the issue and the policy recommendations herein.

Works Cited

Airbnb. (n.d.-a). Airbnb Community. *Airbnb.com*. Retrieved from https://community.withairbnb.com/t5/Community-Center/ct-p/community-center on July 2, 2020.

Airbnb. (n.d.-b). Fast facts. *Airbnb.com*. Retrieved from https://news.airbnb.com/fast-facts/ on June 1, 2020.

Airbnb. (2013). New study: Airbnb generated $632 million in economic activity in New York. *Airbnb.com*. Retrieved from https://www.airbnb.com/press/news/new-study-airbnb-generated-632-million-in-economic-activity-in-new-york on July 2, 2020.

---

[6] On Airbnb's community site for hosts (Airbnb n.d.-a), a search for the term "fake guest" yielded 552 results on May 15, 2020.

[7] Airbnb has been criticized for sending professional photographers to properties to take free listing photos but not conducting safety inspections (Howard 2015).

Airbnb. (2019). Airbnb estimated direct economic impact in the U.S. nears $34 billion. *Airbnb.com*. Retrieved from https://news.airbnb.com/en-us/airbnb-estimated-direct-economic-impact-in-the-u-s-nears-34-billion/ on July 2, 2020.

Braithwaite, J. (1982). Enforced self-regulation: A new strategy for corporate crime control. *Michigan Law Review, 80*(7), 1466. https://doi.org/10.2307/1288556.

Brooks, D. J. (2010). What is security: Definition through knowledge categorization. *Security Journal, 23*(3), 225–239.

CNBC.com Staff. (2019). Disruptor 50 2019: 7. Airbnb. *CNBC.com*. Retrieved from https://www.cnbc.com/2019/05/14/airbnb-2019-disruptor-50.html on July 2, 2020.

Enz, C. A. (2009). The physical safety and security features of U.S. hotels. *Cornell Hospitality Quarterly, 50*(4), 553–560. https://doi.org/10.1177/193896550934596.

Farronato, C., & Fradkin, A. (2018). *The welfare effects of peer entry in the accommodation market: The case of Airbnb*. National Bureau of Economic Research.

Feickert, J., Verma, R., Plaschka, G., & Dev, C. S. (2006). Safeguarding your customers. *Cornell Hotel and Restaurant Administration Quarterly, 47*(3), 224–244. https://doi.org/10.1177/0010880406288872.

Fennelly, L. J. (Ed.). (2016). *Effective physical security*. Butterworth-Heinemann.

Gerdeman, D. (2018). The Airbnb effect: Cheaper rooms for travelers, less revenue for hotels. *Forbes*, February 27. Retrieved from https://www.forbes.com/sites/hbsworkingknowledge/2018/02/27/the-airbnb-effect-cheaper-rooms-for-travelers-less-revenue-for-hotels/#50f86803d672 on July 2, 2020.

Gill, M., Moon, C., Seaman, P., & Turbin, V. (2002). Security management and crime in hotels. *International Journal of Contemporary Hospitality Management, 14*(2), 58–64. https://doi.org/10.1108/09596110210419237.

Gottfredson, M. R., & Hirschi, T. (1995). National crime control policies. *Society, 32*, 30–36. https://doi.org/10.1007/BF02693290.

Griswold, A. (2016). You can rent an entire home on Airbnb for the price of a hotel room in the US. *Quartz*, September 16. Retrieved from https://qz.com/779121/airbnb-vs-hotel-cost-comparison-you-can-rent-an-entire-home-on-airbnb-for-the-price-of-a-hotel-room/ on July, 2, 2020.

Groenenboom, K., & Jones, P. (2003). Issues of security in hotels. *International Journal of Contemporary Hospitality Management, 15*(1), 14–19.

Herbert, S. (1999). The end of the territorially-sovereign state? The case of crime control in the United States. *Political Geography, 18*(2), 149–172. https://doi.org/10.1016/s0962-6298(98)00080-8.

Howard, A. (2015). A man died at an airbnb rental. Here's how the company responded. *Huff Post*, November 10. Retrieved from https://www.huffpost.com/entry/a-death-at-an-airbnb-rental-puts-the-tech-company-in-the-hot-seat_n_5640db66e4b0b24aee4b18f7 on July 2, 2020.

Hua, N., & Yang, Y. (2017). Systematic effects of crime on hotel operating performance. *Tourism Management, 60*, 257–269. https://doi.org/10.1016/j.tourman.2016.11.022.

Lisante, T. W. (1972). Improving hotel security. *The Cornell H.R. Quarterly, 13*(1), 2–10.

Magalhães, M. J., de Magalhães, S. T., Revett, K., & Jahankhani, H. (2017). A review on privacy issues in hotels: A contribution to the definition of information security policies and marketing strategies. In *International conference on global security, safety, and sustainability* (pp. 205–217). Springer.

Marzen, C., Prum, D. A., & Alberts, R. J. (2017). The new sharing economy: The role of property, tort, and contract law for managing the airbnb model. *New York University Journal of Law and Business, 13*(2), 295–336.

McNamara, B. (2015). Airbnb: A not-so-safe resting place. *Colorado Technology Law Journal, 13*(1), 149–170.

Much Needed. (2020). Airbnb by the numbers: Usage, demographics, and revenue growth. *Muchneeded.com*. Retrieved from https://muchneeded.com/airbnb-statistics/ on July 2, 2020.

Mudallal, Z. (2015). Airbnb will soon be booking more rooms than the world's largest hotel chains. *Quartz*, January 20. Retrieved from https://qz.com/329735/airbnb-will-soon-be-booking-more-rooms-than-the-worlds-largest-hotel-chains/ on July 2, 2020.

Oxford Economics. (2019). Economic impact of the U.S. hotel industry. *www.ahla.com*. Retrieved from https://www.ahla.com/sites/default/files/oxford2019.pdf on July 2, 2020.

Palombo, D. (2015). A tale of two cities: The regulatory battle to incorporate short-term residential rentals into modern law. *American University Business Law Review, 4*, 287–321.

World Travel and Tourism Council. (2020). Economic impact reports. *wttc.org*. Retrieved from https://wttc.org/Research/Economic-Impact#:~:text=US%248.9%20trillion%20contribution%20to,28.3%25%20of%20global%20services%20exports on July 2, 2020.

Chapter 2
What Is Home Sharing in Relation to the Hospitality Industry?

Deciding where to stay when sleeping away from home is complicated by the newest, cost-effective competitor in travel and tourism, home sharing. Part of the new gig economy, home sharing is literally when someone has a *home*, or part of a home, they are not using that they make available to *share* with members of the public looking for a place to stay. The hosts and the guests find each other through the website of a home-sharing company, such as Airbnb, VRBO, or HomeAway. The guests pay the hosts for their stay, usually at prices that are competitive with or more economical than local hotel rates, and the home-sharing company gets a percentage.

Home sharing has become a popular option worldwide, even though risks to users of home-sharing sites, including hosts and guests, are becoming more clear. The fact is that users are not likely aware of the extent to which their vulnerability to unsafe or unsecure situations may be heightened. Further, users are neither granted the same legal protection nor have the same legal responsibilities as when staying at a hotel. Hotels offer public accommodations that are among the most highly regulated of any private business, ensuring accountability for safety and security, as well as nondiscrimination, access, and other public values. By contrast, as will be explored in future chapters, home sharing is almost entirely unregulated; accountability for safety and security is left to users to manage.

2.1 The Commercial Landscape of Hospitality

The provision of a safe and secure place to sleep to a stranger is an ancient practice. But what was once a neighborly action has grown into a big business. Take, for example, three of the biggest hotel providers in the world in order: Marriott International, Hilton Worldwide Holdings, and InterContinental Hotel Group.

C. A. Binns, R. J. Kempf, *Safety and Security in Hotels and Home Sharing*, SpringerBriefs in Criminology, https://doi.org/10.1007/978-3-030-59306-3_2

Table 2.1 Three large hotel providers' revenue, properties, rooms, and brands worldwide (2019)

Corporate name	Gross revenue	Number of properties	Number of rooms	Example brands
Marriott International	$20.97 billion	7349	1,380,921	Marriott, Fairfield Inn and Suites, Sheraton, Westin
Hilton Worldwide Holdings Inc.	$9.45 billion	6103	971,780	Hilton Hotels and Resorts, Hampton, Doubletree, Waldorf Astoria
InterContinental Hotels Group	$2.08 billion	5885	70,981	Holiday Inn, Candlewood Suites, Klimton, Crowne Plaza

Sources: Marriott International (2019); Hilton Worldwide Holdings Inc (2019); InterContinental Hotels Group (2019).

Table 2.1 compares these companies on several measures and shows that this is a multibillion dollar industry worldwide.

Home sharing has likewise become an important, worldwide business, albeit not as big a revenue driver as the hotel corporations listed above. The meteoric rise in home sharing might be a bit surprising because the concept has only been around since 2007; however, the growth has been assisted with the vast proliferation of Internet access and competitive prices. As a result, the spread of the home-sharing concept as an alternative to staying at hotels has impacted hotel revenue. It has been estimated that hotels annually lose $450 million in revenue because of Airbnb alone (Lewis 2019). Although there are several home-sharing companies, details are provided here about Airbnb.

Airbnb The concept of home sharing through the Internet began in 2007 when three friends in San Francisco offered air mattresses to out-of-town conference attendees who could not find other accommodations. This experience gave them the idea to connect people who had needs for short term stays with others who had room to rent. They first named their company "AirBed and Breakfast," referring to the air mattresses they employed, but later shortened it to Airbnb (Aydin 2019).

Since its launch, the company has provided a home-sharing platform for more than 150 million users, hosting over 400 million guests worldwide (Much Needed 2020). Airbnb is present in more than 190 countries (Much Needed 2020), and on any given night, an average of more than two million people stay in an Airbnb property (Airbnb n.d.). Airbnb's most popular international destinations in 2019 were Kaikoura, New Zealand; Xiamen, China; Puebla, Mexico; and Normandy, France (Rosen 2018).

In the United States, Airbnb stays are on average less costly than hotels on average. For example, in 2019, US Airbnb guests stayed 4.3 days and, per night, paid $141, although these averages skew high with the median stay having been 3 days and the median Airbnb rate having been $102 (Pillow n.d.). That said, prices vary greatly depending on where the Airbnb property is located. Table 2.2 presents 2015 data collected by Busbud that compares the average price of Airbnb rooms in major

Table 2.2 Price comparison of Airbnbs and hotels (2015)

City	Average pice of an Airbnb property	Average price of a hotel room
Chicago	$150	$179
New York	$164	$245
New Orleans	$201	$191
San Francisco	$221	$217

Source: Busbud (2016)

US cities to the average price of hotels.[1] It shows that in some places, airbnb rental actually costs more than hotels at that time.

Airbnb earns its revenue in two ways (Nath 2020). First, the company collects a 3% service fee from hosts for each completed booking, i.e., all bookings that are not canceled by the host. In addition, the company collects a nonrefundable fee from guests upon booking, which varies depending on the size of the reservation and type of property but is usually not more than 14.2%. This adds up significant revenue, although the total is unknown because as a private company, Airbnb does not have to report such numbers. That said, Airbnb's revenue has gotten attention since the company announced it was considering an initial public offering (IPO) of stock in 2020 (Tweedy and Holmes 2019). According to the Wall Street Journal, in 2017, it was valued at $31 billion, but posted a net loss of $322 million in the first three quarters of 2019 (Eaglesham et al. 2020). Further, it is very likely Airbnb has been negatively impacted by the COVID-19 pandemic, and the IPO seems uncertain at the time (Walker 2020). Further discussion of COVID-19 and home shares can be found in an upcoming chapter.

Pandemic aside, Airbnb is not the only entity earning money from home sharing. According to Airbnb, in terms of revenue, the average host with one property listed makes about $7200 a year sharing their home on Airbnb. Airbnb reported that worldwide, in 2019, there were approximately 6 million listings globally (Airbnb 2019). Of these, about one-third of hosts, approximately 2 million, rent out a single property, but one-third, another 2 million, rent out between two to twenty-four properties, and the final 2 million rent out 25 or more properties. Statistically speaking, in the United States, multiunit entire-home hosts have been the fastest-growing Airbnb segment in terms of the number of hosts, units, and revenue generated in 2016 (CBRE 2017). Entire-home units made up 81% of the US hosts' revenue.

2.2 Conclusion

In a very short time, home sharing has become an important element of the hospitality industry. Further, it provides a new way for individuals to earn money from their homes. Nevertheless, there are implications to home sharing related to the safety

[1] The sources of Busbud's data were Inside Airbnb and Hotels.com

and security of hosts and guests that need to be examined. To shed light on these problems, the next chapter explores available crime data.

Works Cited

Airbnb. (2019). Airbnb hosts share more than six million listings around the world. *Airbnb.com*. Retrieved April 12, 2019 from https://news.airbnb.com/airbnb-hosts-share-more-than-six-million-listings-around-the-world/ on July 2, 2020.

Airbnb. (n.d.). Fast facts. *Airbnb.com*. Retrieved from https://news.airbnb.com/fast-facts/ on June 1, 2020.

Aydin, R. (2019). How 3 guys turned renting mattresses in their apartment into a $31 billion company, Airbnb. *Business Insider*, September 20. Retrieved from https://www.businessinsider.com/how-airbnb-was-founded-a-visual-history-2016-2 on July 2, 2020.

Busbud. (2016). Comparing Airbnb and hotel rates around the globe. *www.busbud.com*. Retrieved from https://www.busbud.com/blog/airbnb-vs-hotel-rates/ on July 2, 2020.

CBRE. (2017). Hosts with multiple units – A key driver of Airbnb growth – A comprehensive national review including a spotlight on 13 U.S. markets. *www.ahla.com*. Retrieved from https://www.ahla.com/hosts-multiple-units-key-driver-airbnb-growth on July 2, 2020.

Eaglesham, J., Farrell, M., & Grind, K. (2020). Airbnb swings to a loss as costs climb ahead of IPO. *The Wall Street Journal*, June 28. Retrieved from https://www.wsj.com/articles/airbnb-swings-to-a-loss-as-costs-climb-ahead-of-ipo-11581443123 on July 2, 2020.

Hilton Worldwide Holdings Inc. (2019). Form 10-K.

InterContinental Hotels Group. (2019). Annual report. *IHGPLC*. Retrieved from https://www.ihgplc.com/investors/annual-report?tab=right on 7/2/2020.

Lewis, T. (2019). Airbnb statistics growth, revenue, hosts + more! *www.hostsorter.com*. Retrieved from www.hostsorter.com/airbnb-statistics/ on July 2, 2020.

Marriott International. (2019). *Form 10-K*.

Much Needed. (2020). Airbnb by the numbers: Usage, demographics, and revenue growth. *Muchneeded.com*. Retrieved from https://muchneeded.com/airbnb-statistics/ on July 2, 2020.

Nath, T. (2020). How Airbnb makes money. *Investopedia,* March 30. Retrieved from https://www.investopedia.com/articles/investing/112414/how-airbnb-makes-money.asp on July 2, 2020.

Pillow. (n.d.). Crunching the numbers: Defining 'normal' for Airbnb hosts and listings. *pillow.com*. Retrieved from https://blog.pillow.com/crunching-the-numbers-defining-normal-for-airbnb-hosts-and-listings/ on June 1, 2020.

Rosen, E. (2018). Airbnb ranks the world's top destinations for 2019. *Forbes,* December 10. Retrieved from www.forbes.com/sites/ericrosen/2018/12/10/airbnb-ranks-the-worlds-top-destinations-for-2019/#6e92089e1138 on July 2, 2020.

Tweedy, S., & Holmes, A. (2019). $31 billion Airbnb announces plan to go public in 2020. *Business Insider*, September 19. Retrieved from https://www.businessinsider.com/airbnb-announces-plan-to-go-public-in-2020-ipo-2019-9 on June 2, 2020.

Walker, R. (2020). Will Airbnb and other IPO hopefuls still go public in the middle of a pandemic? *Marker*, March 23. Retrieved from https://marker.medium.com/will-airbnb-and-other-ipo-hopefuls-still-go-public-in-the-middle-of-a-pandemic-32d63a4dcfb4 on July 2, 2020.

Chapter 3
What Do We Learn from the Crime and Safety Data on Home Shares?

Murder *In November 2018, for five days, a woman stayed in an Airbnb in Costa Rica for her thirty-fifth birthday. She was accompanied by a family member except for the final day of her stay, when she spent the night alone. It was this final night when she met a dark fate, despite having chosen an Airbnb that was close to the airport, located in a safe neighborhood, and protected by a security guard. She remained in regular contact with a friend whom she was to meet in Florida at the end of her trip; however, she never made it to the Costa Rican airport. A week later, the woman's body was found less than 200 feet away from her rental, "half-buried and wrapped in plastic in a patch of forest." She had a broken neck, stab wounds, and blunt force trauma to her head. Investigators believe the crime was sexually motivated. On the day she went missing, her Airbnb was already being cleaned and new guests checked in. Ultimately, the security guard for her Airbnb, who lived next door, confessed to the crime, which was corroborated by DNA evidence* (Specia and Mzezewa 2019; Fieldstadt 2020; O'Connell 2020; Madan 2018).

Accidental Death *In November 2013, Zak Stone's family rented an Airbnb in Austin, TX, for a Thanksgiving family gathering. One of the features that attracted them to the property was the inviting rope swing in the garden. Unbeknownst to the Stones, the tree holding the swing was dead. On Thanksgiving day, Zak Stone's father went outside to enjoy a ride on that swing, when the tree holding it suddenly snapped and fell on his head, causing severe brain damage, which ultimately killed him. Following his father's death, Mr. Stone did not pursue legal action against Airbnb, but has been openly critical of their safety procedures. His family ultimately reached a settlement with the host's insurance company* (Newton 2015; Stone 2016; Lieber 2015b; Howard 2015).

It is one thing to say that there are potential safety and security issues in home sharing. It is another to measure the extent to which these problems actually occur

C. A. Binns, R. J. Kempf, *Safety and Security in Hotels and Home Sharing*, SpringerBriefs in Criminology, https://doi.org/10.1007/978-3-030-59306-3_3

in this setting. This type of crime analysis is critical in identifying security risks and designing security measures. The first step is to identify the relevant crimes that occur. Then, these crimes are analyzed to determine levels of risk and to design security methods to help prevent the crimes from occurring.

Yet, a crime analysis of home sharing, as well as of hotels, presents challenges. Clear measures of the types of crimes happening in these settings are difficult to find. Over 20 years ago, researchers pointed out that there was insufficient data to carefully study hotel crime (Huang et al. 1998) and that has not changed today, although in one 2009 study, it was determined that most hotel crimes were property-related (Xu et al. 2017). The US Bureau of Justice Statistics collects some data about hotel crime with its National Crime Victims Survey (NCVS), but these data are both limited and dated. There is no other known centralized source of available official crime or safety data for hotels.

Likewise, there is scant publicly-available data regarding home-sharing crime. In 2014, a New York Times journalist requested data about safety statistics directly from Airbnb, but Airbnb declined to provide it, citing privacy reasons (Lieber 2014). (He also asked hotels for their "death rate," which was not provided either.) Further, home-sharing security has not yet received a lot of attention in scholarly literature (Gill et al. 2002).

Available studies are generally critical of home sharing, expressing security concerns (Han and Wang 2019; Xu et al. 2017). Xu et al. (2017) examined Airbnb and crime. Their media analysis demonstrated that guests of the Airbnb rentals have (1) been targets of crime, (2) had valuables stolen while staying at these properties, and (3) may in fact be more exposed to a greater range of crimes due to not being in a tourist location. They also found a significant spatial relationship between Airbnb and the crimes of robbery, motor vehicle theft, and property crime. Their study also determined that shared rooms were positively related to crime.

The results of Han and Wang's (2019) study suggested that a reduction in Airbnb listings in an area leads to a reduction in crime. They also found that increased Airbnb activity in neighborhoods with high median incomes, higher housing prices, and lower unemployment rate are likely to have increased crime. There was a silver lining that came out of Han and Wang's study (2019). They investigated the heterogeneous effects of Airbnb occupancy on different types of neighborhoods and learned that in neighborhoods with lower income, housing price, and population, Airbnb activity may actually result in decreased crime. This is because in those communities, Airbnb supply may improve local economic conditions and thereby reduce the number of potential offenders.

While the above research provides helpful information, anecdotal evidence is necessary to further understand the risks sleeping away from home (Lieber 2014). This research sets out to provide broad measures of the problems that occur in hotels and home shares. First, security concerns are addressed below. Then, safety concerns are examined.

3.1 Security Concerns in Hotels and Home Shares

The NCVS is an annual survey of a nationally representative sample of crime victims, consisting of about 160,000 unique persons in about 95,000 households about their personal demographics and experience with crime (Bureau of Justice Statistics 2018). The most recent NCVS report summarizes data collected in 2018, but notably, after 2008, the Bureau of Justice Statistics decided to aggregate crimes occurring in homes with crimes occurring in hotels or vacation homes. For example, in the 2018 report, the crime of "burglary/trespassing" includes "forcible entry or attempted entry of places, including a permanent residence, other residence (e.g., a *hotel room or vacation residence*), or other structure (e.g., a garage or shed). Includes victimizations where the offender stole, attempted to steal, or did not attempt to steal. Does not include trespassing on land" (Morgan and Oudekerk 2018, p. 5). Therefore, when the report notes that burglary/trespassing has increased from 20.6 per 1000 families in 2017 to 21.1 per 1000 families in 2018, there is no way to know what percentage of these rates is attributable to hotels or home shares.

The last year the NCVS collected specific data about hotel crime was 2008. In that report, violent victimizations are broken out by the location where it occurred, including a victim's own dwelling, attached garage, or enclosed porch; a detached building on a victim's own property; in the victim's vacation or second home; and in the victim's hotel or motel room. The average annual number of *violent* victimizations in hotel or motel rooms from 2004 to 2008 was 0.1% of the total (Bureau of Justice Statistics 2008). The average annual number of *property* victimizations in hotel or motel rooms for the same period was 0.3%. In each case, the crime rate was lower in hotel and motel rooms than in the other locations.

For home shares, the data are even less readily available, although criminals, posing as both guests and hosts, are known to use home-sharing properties specifically to conduct crime. For example, police from Toronto, Canada, have reported increases in cases of human trafficking in home shares. They suspect these crimes have been occurring in this setting because individuals can be more anonymous than in a hotel, which makes it harder to investigate (McIntosh 2018). Table 3.1 lists a sample of crimes reported to have occurred in home share settings that the authors identified from available media reports published between 2015 and 2020. The crimes are sorted by type of victim: home-sharing guest or host. A rate of crime per home-sharing user is not calculable; however, these crimes are not minor in nature.

Unique Crimes in the Home-Sharing Setting

A review of anecdotal data shows that several types of crimes are unique to the home-sharing environment. This section provides case studies highlighting two of these crimes: fake listings, illegal listings. It also discusses the issue of using a home share to conduct illegal behavior.

Table 3.1 Crimes reported to have occurred in home shares (2015–2020)

Type of victim	Crime type	Description
Guest	Assault	Host assaulted a guest (McCleary 2016)
Guest	Discrimination	Host discriminated against guest (Bella 2019)
Guest	Harassment	Host harassed a guest by sending threatening messages (Kircher 2016)
Guest	Illegal videotaping	Host placed hidden cameras in property without guests' consent (Golgowski 2017; Rivas 2019)
Guest	Kidnapping	Host kidnapped a guest (Lieber 2015a)
Guest	Murder	Host murdered a guest (Specia and Mzezewa 2019)
Guest	Pedophile host	Convicted pedophiles posted rooms and marketed them to young children (French 2017)
Guest	Prostitution	Guest booked a room that was inside an illegal brothel operated by the host (Fasick and Golding 2016)
Guest	Rape and murder	Host raped and murdered guest (Hannam 2017; Syfret 2017)
Guest	Sexual harassment	Host sexually harassed a guest (Lieber 2015a)
Guest	Illegal listing	Host posted a room located in a public housing facility in NYC (Ferré-Sadurní 2019a, b)
Guest and host	Hacking	Airbnb accounts have been hacked resulting in money loss to both guests and hosts (Villasanta 2019)
Host	Child sex assault	A guest sexually assaulted the host's child (Marie Claire 2017)
Host	Drug use and vandalism	Guests left behind drugs, knives, and bloodstains at host's property (Hollan 2020)
Host	Drugs use and manufacturing	Guest operated a drug lab in home share (Thomas-Wilson and Lim 2019)
Host	Harassment	Guest harassed and threatened host (Hohman 2018)
Host	Illegal event	Guest held large party in violation of COVID-19 regulations (Campbell and Redick 2020)
Host	Illegal event	Guest hosted an orgy in the host's property (Yuhas 2015)
Host	Illegal event; illegal gun use	Guest fired guns on property, during illegal party (Vadaj 2020)
Host	Prostitution	Guest used a host's apartment to engage in illegal prostitution (Sauchelli and Golding 2014)
Host	Squatting	Guests turn to squatters, refusing to vacate home after home sharing has ended (Fokos 2015)
Host	Theft	Guest stole contents of host's home (Bench 2019)
Host	Vandalism	Guest vandalized host's property (Tikader 2020)

Source: Authors' research

Fake Listings and Other Frauds When you book a hotel room from a hotel's website, the process is very straightforward. You look at room options and price points. Many hotel websites offer pictures of the room and list the amenities. You pay for the room based on the type of accommodation you seek – generally speaking, smaller rooms without views and less amenities cost less, while larger rooms with more amenities and views cost more. When booking a hotel room, a guest will never view a fake listing, and very rarely does a hotel overbook. The room you book belongs to the hotel, and that is the room you receive. When you arrive at the hotel, if you do not like the room, you can usually switch to a room you prefer without penalty, unless you decide you want a room with more features, which might cost more money.

With home sharing, the same general process happens. You view possible rooms and amenities of several properties online and make a selection according to your preference and budget. However, when you book a room on home-sharing sites, there is a risk that your room will not be as advertised. Perhaps the room might not even exist. There have been many cases of this kind of bait and switch reported by users of Airbnb on Reddit at r/Airbnb, the website Airbnbhell.com, among other places.

In addition to bait and switch schemes, there are several other reported scams, which are unique to home sharing. Several are presented in Table 3.2. As the table shows, most of these cases negatively affect guests, suggesting that they are more vulnerable than hosts.

Another related issue arises when a host contacts a guest and asks the guest to change their selection at the last minute, at a point when it is too late to explore other options (Kukura 2020; Finn 2020; Merlan 2020). This type of change is allowed by Airbnb's policy under an "unavoidable circumstance" clause for "unforeseen property damage, maintenance, and amenity issues" (Kukura 2020). Chances are, the property originally selected never existed in the first place (Kukura 2020; Merlan 2020). If the property is one advertised on Airbnb, if you stay just one night in the substituted location, in addition to making yourself vulnerable to safety and security problems, you risk eligibility to collect a full refund for the change per Airbnb policy. Some hosts exploit Airbnb's refund policy in this way to ensure payment regardless of a guest's initial choice of property (Conti 2019).

One user's experience with an "unavoidable circumstance" exposed a massive fraud wherein hosts employed "phony listings," "fake reviews," and "intimidation," which spanned eight cities and affected over 100 listed Airbnb properties (Conti 2019). This guest became a victim of this scam after booking a room with a host who contacted her at the last minute to switch rooms due to a "plumbing issue." The host claimed the new room was even better than the original one. The guest agreed to the change and accepted on the Airbnb app; however, the new property ended up being a substandard accommodation, with a fake address. The guest described the substitute accommodations as a "flophouse," but without alternate plans, she stayed the evening. The next day, the host contacted her again, insisting she had to leave. She booked a hotel room for the remainder of her stay.

After this difficult experience, the host boldly reached out to the guest to request "no less than a five star review." (Conti 2019) Meanwhile, the guest sought a refund for the cost of her booking which was $1221.20. Ultimately, she was refunded only 33% of her original payment – $399. The host retained the remainder. The reason for this financial penalty was that Airbnb rules disqualify guests from receiving full

Table 3.2 Frauds reported to have occurred in home shares

Scam	Description
Asking a guest to cancel their booking	This tactic is highly advantageous to the host, because in the event of a strict cancellation policy, when the guest cancels after a certain period, they will forfeit 50% of the rental fee to the host, for never having stayed at the property (Johnson 2017)
Bogus damage charges	Hosts will claim the guests damaged something during their stay and seek "reimbursement" (Kukura 2020)
Deleting negative reviews	Hosts will submit fake "evidence" to the home-sharing company to get a guest's review deleted (Kukura 2020; Merlan 2020)
Double booking a property	Guests will book a listed house thinking they have the entire house to themselves, yet when they arrive, additional guests are present. Sometimes this is due to the listing being presented on multiple platforms (Merlan 2020).
Extorting positive reviews	Hosts, especially superhosts who must maintain a 4.8-star average, are under tremendous pressure to maintain high ratings. Thus, hosts demand a five-star review, regardless of the guest's experience, or host only book guests who have ranked other hosts with five stars (Kukura 2020; Merlan 2020)
Harassment and/or retaliation for negative reviews	Hosts will contact a guest personally to complain about their negative review and perhaps make personal threats in order to compel the edit or removal of the review (Merlan 2020)
Listing the same property on different home-sharing sites at different prices	The property is listed on multiple platforms, such as Airbnb, Home Away, and VRBO, at multiple price points. The host will take the booking with the guests who are willing to pay the highest price (Kukura 2020).
Paying outside the Airbnb app	Hosts try to get guests to pay outside of the home-sharing platform so they can save on fees. This is not recommended, because the guest will not have any protection from the company under these circumstances (Airbnb n.d.; Kukura 2020; Merlan 2020))
Property-related scams	A guest does something to damage the property, such as smoke in the home share, break an item, lose or steal the keys, or steal an item, and denies it (Kukura 2020; Merlan 2020)
Stalling a refund	Airbnb only provides a 2-week window to leave a review. If a host stalls providing a refund, that period can be exhausted preventing a guest from writing a bad review (Kukura 2020; Merlan 2020)

Source: Authors' Research

refunds if they stay at least one night at a host's property. This was true even though the host contacted her at the last minute, and it was not convenient for her to stay anywhere else. Angered by "poorly written rules" on the part of Airbnb, the guest investigated the host. She found that the same host, using different host names including "Kris and Becky," "Kelsey and Jean," "Alex and Brittany," and "Becky and Andrew," posted the same exact listing in several states with varying prices posting pictures using different camera angles of the same property. The host was profiting off of this scam because as guests were manipulated to stay on day on a substitute property, they could keep most of the money when the guest became ineligible to receive a refund.

Hotels, in contrast, may not collect funds from users who do not receive the room they booked. Hotels may charge a cancellation fee if someone cancels a hotel booking at the last minute, but this is paid by all users equally and is not contingent upon their individual experiences at the hotel. These cancellation rules are also set forth in writing and are made clear to all users; however, Airbnb's rules are more complex and less transparent. The rules give great latitude to the host to select their own refund model, ranging from "flexible" to "super strict" with Airbnb having the "final say in all disputes." (Conti 2019). Additionally, Airbnb is paid their service fee whether someone receives the room they were promised, or not; whether someone has a safe and secure stay, or not.

In home sharing, ideally, online review systems would prevent such scams. Airbnb, in particular, requires both hosts and guests to review one another, which should give future users information about who they are interacting with. However, after experiencing the bait and switch scam described above, the guest suggested that the review system is flawed. Even after being switched to a substandard location and not being able to get a refund for her booking, the host contacted her and asked for a five-star rating to manipulate Airbnb's algorithms (Conti 2019). The host also told her to communicate any concerns privately rather than reflect them in a written review. The guest interpreted this interaction as a "warning" against leaving honest feedback, because of the implied threat that she would not receive a good review as an Airbnb guest. She concluded that this system of dual feedback causes users to avoid confrontation with each other so as not to be retaliated against (Conti 2019). The guest's investigation also found that her host's many positive reviews had been left by other "fake" accounts – all of which she determined were managed by the same person.

Illegal Listings Another variation on fake listings problem relates to the situation when hosts circumvent local laws to share their home. In these cases, the host has no legal authority to share their home, and as a result, the guest's presence is technically illegal. This is not only undermining the rules that the community has set for itself but also presenting a security concern to the community. As described in more detail in Chap. 4, illegal home sharing has been shown to be common in large cities. In New York City, housing laws prohibit the rental of apartments for less than 30 days unless the host is also present (Plautz 2015). Yet, in 2016, the New York Attorney General estimated that 72% of Airbnb rentals in New York City violated these conditions (Schneiderman 2014). Just a year earlier, a New York City Assemblymember went undercover to visit several Airbnb listings in the city to expose what she said was a "pervasive" illegal hotel problem. She found "management companies posing as tenants, landlords converting residential buildings into hotel-style lodging, and one rental company with over 200 listings" (Plautz 2015). In the United Kingdom, an investigation by the Daily Mail estimated that over 120,000 properties were being illegally sublet on Airbnb and were being used to host brothels and raves (Ellery et al. 2018). In these cases, home-sharing guests are, knowingly and unknowingly, contributing to illegal actions in the community.

An extraordinary example, reported in the New York Times, involved a host who listed a property on Airbnb that was located in a New York City public housing development (Ferré-Sadurní 2019a). The case demonstrates the extraordinary and perhaps unrealistic responsibility of the guest in ensuring their listing is legal. In this case, the host was in the wrong, as subletting government-sponsored housing is illegal. The guest was refunded for their booking; however, the guest still experienced hardship due to this incident, as she went so far as to arrive at the property, physically assess the situation, and then hastily seek alternate accommodations. Ultimately, the host is responsible for making sure their property is legally available for home sharing, not the home-sharing company. This means it is up to the guest to research the address, once known, in an effort to proactively avoid booking illegal home shares (Ferré-Sadurní 2019a, b). However, this can be challenging to research in a timely manner, given the current booking practices. Today, guests are not provided the host's address until they book and pay for the property (Airbnb 2020). Ideally, guests would be able to research the listing beforehand, so they could avoid a potentially problematic listing before having to pay for it.

Using the Home Share for Illegal Behavior As shown in Table 3.1, guests have pursued crime in their hosts' homes. There are multiple reports of home-sharing properties being used as illegal brothels (Nyheter 2016; BBC 2017; Berghuis 2018) and drug labs (Seth 2017); to film pornographic videos (Susko and Schrader 2016; Associated Press 2018) and have sex parties (Rosario et al. 2014); and to provide a setting for drug delivery services (Moyer and Hsu 2018) and human trafficking (Marchildon 2018). Private homes provide more privacy for these illegal activities to occur.

Due to these activities, communities where home sharing is occurring experience negative consequences. One example is in the Phoenix area, where homeowners have said home-sharing guests are "wreaking havoc" in their area (Loew 2020). One such homeowner said she "never knows who is going to be staying next door" and that has "affected her ability to feel safe in her own home." (Loew 2020). Many neighbors of home shares around the world have reported feeling unsafe in their homes as a result of the presence of home-sharing guests (Docklands News 2020; Chung 2017; Feith 2019; Foster 2019; Francis and Littleson 2020; Wiśniewska 2019).

Crime concerns in home shares have led at least one major employer to ban their employees from using Airbnb for business travel. In 2019, consulting firm Accenture banned their staff from using the platform after "workers were attacked in a violent burglary" in Stockport, England (Clowes and O'Dwyer 2019), even though Airbnb responded by saying this incident was "incredibly rare." (Clowes and O'Dwyer 2019).

Hotels experience less crime, particularly because staff are trained to identify potential bad actors. For example, the American Hotel and Lodging Association encourages training for hotel employees to help them identify human trafficking. The Association provides free guides and resources for hotels to use for this purpose. Mandatory training requirements vary based on state law. California is a state that specifically requires hotel employees to attend human trafficking training (Yaffe 2019).

3.2 Safety Concerns in Hotels and Home Shares

As is further detailed in Chap. 4, hotels are subject to a number of regulations related to safety, addressing such issues such as fire, tornado, and hurricane. Home sharing is not subject to similar regulations, and therefore, safety precautions are largely voluntary on the part of the hosts. A 2018 study, published in Injury Prevention, explored the safety status of Airbnb properties (Kennedy et al. 2019). The authors examined over 120,000 properties listed on Airbnb in 16 US cities to analyze host-reported safety features. Overall, they found safety deficiencies, including missing smoke detectors (20%), carbon monoxide detectors (42.5%), fire extinguishers (58%), and first aid kits (64%). The researchers concluded "Local and state governments or Airbnb must implement regulations compliant with current National Fire Protection Association (NFPA) fire safety standards" (Kennedy et al. 2019, p. 328).

Following this report, in December 2018, Airbnb announced they were introducing new safety measures. Those measures included a partnership with the American Red Cross (ARC). As part of that partnership, they donated $1 million dollars to the ARC, in support of a campaign where they install free smoke alarms in communities (Airbnb 2018). They also announced an enhancement of their existing program, where they offer free smoke and carbon monoxide detectors to hosts, a program that had existed since 2014 (Airbnb 2018). They also reported increasing their educational resources, creating a Home Safety webpage, and "flagging" listings where smoke and carbon monoxide detectors have not been reported by the host, so guests are "aware" (Airbnb 2018). Nevertheless, unless a locality has imposed requirements, safety measures remain voluntary in home share.

3.3 Conclusion

Although quantifiable data are not currently available to measure crime in home shares, anecdotal evidence proves that this setting is vulnerable to significant crimes and safety issues. Furthermore, new crimes have emerged that are uniquely related to home shares. These crimes include hosts creating fake listings, hosts illegally sharing homes, and guests using home shares to commit illegal acts on another's property. Safety issues are heightened because hosts' adoption of protective measures varies. These issues should provide cause for concern to home-sharing users and policymakers. The current laws and regulations that these safety and security concerns are addressed in the next chapter.

Works Cited

Airbnb. (2018). Airbnb introduces new global measures to help keep people safe. *Airbnb.com*. Retrieved from https://news.airbnb.com/new-safety-measures-2018/ on June 28, 2020.

Airbnb. (2020). Is my listing's address visible on Airbnb? *Airbnb.com*. Retrieved from https://www.airbnb.com/help/article/1502/is-my-listings-address-visible-on-airbnb on June 15, 2020.

Airbnb. (n.d.). What should I do if someone asks me to pay outside of the Airbnb website? *Airbnb.com*. Retrieved from https://www.airbnb.com/help/article/199/what-should-i-do-if-someone-asks-me-to-pay-outside-of-the-airbnb-website on July 4, 2020.

Associated Press. (2018). Woman's sues after rental home was used to shoot pornography. *Associated Press*. Retrieved from https://apnews.com/577f18febd334b18b5c8fa0feacd370c/Woman-sues-after-rental-home-was-used-to-shoot-pornography

BBC. (2017). My Airbnb flat was turned into a popup brothel. *BBC.com*. Retrieved from https://www.bbc.com/news/magazine-39528479

Bella, T. (2019). Which monkey is gonna stay on the couch?: Airbnb host kicks out black guests in racist exchange. *The Washington Post*. Retrieved from https://www.washingtonpost.com/nation/2019/06/03/airbnb-racism-host-monkey-black-men-new-york/

Bench, A. (2019). Edmonton police looking for man after furniture and electronics stolen from damaged Airbnb property. *Global News*. Retrieved from https://globalnews.ca/news/6135205/edmonton-airbnb-rental-theft-martin-irwin/

Berghuis, K. (2018). Couple who rented out home as Airbnb found it covered in mystery stains after it was 'used as brothel' *Mirror UK*. Retrieved from https://www.mirror.co.uk/news/uk-news/couple-who-rented-out-home-12978844

Bureau of Justice Statistics. (2008). National crime victimization survey data. *BJS*. Retrieved from https://www.bjs.gov/index.cfm?ty=tp&tid=44 on July 2, 2020.

Bureau of Justice Statistics. (2018). Data collection: National crime victimization survey (NCVS). *BJF*. Retrieved from https://www.bjs.gov/index.cfm?ty=dcdetail&iid=245 on July 2, 2020.

Campbell, & Redick. (2020). Columbus police shut down 2 parties violating stay-at-home order and recover stolen guns. *ABC6*. Retrieved from https://abc6onyourside.com/news/local/columbus-police-shut-down-2-partys-violating-stay-at-home-order-and-recover-stolen-guns

Chung, F. (2017). Residents powerless to stop Airbnb 'partyhouses.' *The Queensland Times*. Retrieved from https://www.qt.com.au/news/residents-powerless-stop-airbnb-party-houses/3192741/

Clowes, E., & O'Dwyer, M. (2019). Accenture bans staff from staying in Airbnb homes after violent burglary. *telegraph.co.uk*, December 7. Retrieved from https://advance-lexis-com.ez.lib.jjay.cuny.edu/api/document?collection=news&id=urn:contentItem:5XP1-7WK1-JCJY-G3NK-00000-00&context=1516831 on July 2, 2020.

Conti, A. (2019). I accidentally uncovered a nationwide scam on Airbnb. *Vice.com*. Retrieved from https://www.vice.com/en_us/article/43k7z3/nationwide-fake-host-scam-on-airbnb

Docklands News. (2020). We live here. *Docklands News*, March 2020. Retrieved from: https://www.docklandsnews.com.au/columns/detail/we-live-here-march-2020_16142/

Ellery, B., Powell, M., & Atkinson, A. (2018). How Airbnb bandits rent out properties to prostitutes, drug dealers and party animals. *Dailymail.com*, December 30. Retrieved from https://www.dailymail.co.uk/news/article-6538881/How-Airbnb-bandits-rent-properties-prostitutes-drug-dealers-party-animals.html on July 4, 2020.

Fasick, K., & Golding, B. (2016). My Airbnb rental turned out to be a secret brothel. *New York Post*, September 8. Retrieved from https://nypost.com/2016/09/07/my-airbnb-rental-turned-out-to-be-a-secret-brothel/ on July 3, 2020.

Feith, J. (2019). Montreal condo complex hires private investigator to catch illegal Airbnb rentals. *Montreal Gazette*. Retrieved from https://montrealgazette.com/news/montreal-condo-complex-hires-private-investigator-to-catch-illegal-airbnb-rentals

Ferré-Sadurní, L. (2019a). Chelsea apartment! Only $90 a night! (Ignore the NYCHA sign). *New York Times*, November 9. Retrieved from https://www.nytimes.com/2019/11/09/nyregion/airbnb-new-york-nycha.html on July 3, 2020.

Ferré-Sadurní, L. (2019b). Inside the rise and fall of a multimillion-dollar Airbnb scheme. *New York Times,* February 23. Retrieved from https://www.nytimes.com/2019/02/23/nyregion/airbnb-nyc-law.html on July 3, 2020.

Fieldstadt, E. (2020). Man convicted of killing Florida woman at Costa Rica Airbnb sentenced to 16 years. *NBC News*, February 18. Retrieved from https://www.nbcnews.com/news/us-news/man-convicted-killing-florida-woman-costa-rica-airbnb-sentenced-16-n1138026 on July 3, 2020.

Finn, J. (2020). Airbnb scams and how to avoid them. *Screenrant*, February 04. Retrieved from https://screenrant.com/how-to-avoid-airbnb-scams/ on July 4, 2020.

Fokos, B. (2015). When your Airbnb guest won't leave. *San Diego Reader*. Retrieved from https://www.sandiegoreader.com/news/2015/sep/09/feature-when-your-airbnb-guest-wont-leave/

Foster, A. (2019). Some Charlotte residents say they want to see more regulations for Airbnb rentals. *3 WBTV*. Retrieved from https://www.wbtv.com/2019/11/06/some-charlotte-residents-say-they-want-see-more-regulations-airbnb-rentals/

Francis, B., & Littleson, R. (2020). More short stay abuse with no recourse for residents. *CBD News*. Retrieved from https://cbdnews.com.au/more-short-stay-abuse-with-no-recourse-for-residents/

French, K. (2017). Revealed: Airbnb host, 23, who advertised Harry Potter-inspired cupboard under the stairs to youngsters is a paedophile who was jailed for attacking children as young as 12. *Daily Mail*. Retrieved from https://www.dailymail.co.uk/news/article-4502336/Harry-Potter-Airbnb-host-revealed-convicted-paedophile.html

Gill, M., Moon, C., Seaman, P., & Turbin, V. (2002). Security management and crime in hotels. *International Journal of Contemporary Hospitality Management, 14*(2), 58–64. https://doi.org/10.1108/09596110210419237.

Golgowski, N. (2017). Couple uncovers hidden cameras in nightmare Airbnb stay: Police. *Huffington Post*, October 11. Retrieved from https://www.huffpost.com/entry/hidden-cameras-airbnb-florida_n_59dd3171e4b01df09b76f949 on July 3, 2020.

Han, W., & Wang, X. (2019). Does home sharing impact crime rate? A tale of two cities. *Proceedings of the International Conference on Information Systems*, Munich, Germany. Retrieved from https://aisel.aisnet.org/icis2019/sustainable_is/sustainable_is/6/ on July 3, 2020.

Hannam, K. (2017). Airbnb hosts in Australia charged with raping and murdering their guest. *Fortune,* October 30. Retrieved from https://fortune.com/2017/10/30/airbnb-murder-melbourne/ on July 4, 2020.

Hohman, M. (2018). Airbnb host claims nightmare guest raided locked bedroom, harassed her: 'I could've been murdered.' *People.com*. Retrieved from https://people.com/home/airbnb-guest-arrested-for-trespassing-host-says-he-harassed-her/

Hollan, M. (2020). Airbnb renter says couple left behind drugs, knives – And bloodstains. *New York Post*. Retrieved from https://nypost.com/2020/02/21/airbnb-renter-says-couple-left-behind-drugs-knives-and-bloodstains/

Howard, A. (2015). A man died at an Airbnb rental. Here's how the company responded. *Huff Post*, November 10. Retrieved from https://www.huffpost.com/entry/a-death-at-an-airbnb-rental-puts-the-tech-company-in-the-hot-seat_n_5640db66e4b0b24aee4b18f7 on July 2, 2020.

Huang, W. S. W., Kwag, M., & Streib, G. (1998). Exploring the relationship between hotel characteristics and crime. *Hospitality Review, 1*(16), Article 9. Retrieved from https://digitalcommons.fiu.edu/hospitalityreview/vol16/iss1/9 on July 3, 2020.

Johnson, S. (2017). Watch out for this tricky Airbnb scam. *The Computer Tutor*. Retrieved from https://computertutorflorida.com/2017/08/watch-out-for-this-tricky-airbnb-scam/

Kennedy, H., et al. (2019). Reported fire safety and first-aid amenities in Airbnb venues in 16 American cities. *Injury Prevention, 25*, 328–330.

Kircher, M. (2016). Racist Airbnb host banned for harassing female grad student. *NY Magazine, Intelligencer*. Retrieved from https://nymag.com/intelligencer/2016/06/racist-airbnb-host-banned-for-harassing-female-grad-student.html

Kukura, J. (2020). Top 10 Airbnb scams bamboozling users out of money across the world. *SFist*, February 5. Retrieved from https://sfist.com/2020/02/04/top-10-airbnb-scams-bamboozling-users-out-of-money-across-the-world/ on July 4, 2020.

Lieber, R. (2014). A liability risk for Airbnb hosts. *New York Times*, December 5. Retrieved from https://www.nytimes.com/2014/12/06/your-money/airbnb-offers-homeowner-liability-coverage-but-hosts-still-have-risks.html on July 3, 2020.

Lieber, R. (2015a). Airbnb horror story points to need for precautions. *New York Times*, August 14. Retrieved from https://www.nytimes.com/2015/08/15/your-money/airbnb-horror-story-points-to-need-for-precautions.html on July 3, 2020.

Lieber, R. (2015b). Death in Airbnb rental raises liability questions. *New York Times,* November 13. Retrieved from https://www.nytimes.com/2015/11/14/your-money/death-in-airbnb-rental-raises-liability-questions.html on July, 2020.

Loew, M. (2020). Some Phoenix-area homeowners say short-term rentals wreaking havoc on their neighborhoods. *AZFamily.com*. Retrieved from https://www.azfamily.com/news/investigations/cbs_5_investigates/some-phoenix-area-homeowners-say-short-term-rentals-wreaking-havoc-on-their-neighborhoods/article_7e3d17c6-5912-11ea-8f40-57069787b6ff.html

Madan, M. O. (2018). Family of Florida woman killed in Costa Rica sues Airbnb. *Miami Herald,* December 22. Retrieved from https://www.miamiherald.com/news/local/article223476120.html on July 3, 2020.

Marchildon, J. (2018). Airbnb rentals are increasingly being used for human trafficking, police say. *Global Citizen*, February 23. Retrieved from www.globalcitizen.org/en/content/airbnb-human-trafficking/ on July 3, 2020.

Marie Claire. (2017). Female guest to sue Airbnb after assault allegations. *Marieclaire.com*. Retrieved from https://www.marieclaire.com.au/airbnb-guest-files-lawsuit-sexual-assault-allegations

McCleary, N. (2016). AirBnB assault suspect is Cumberland County high school teacher. *The Fayetteville Observer*, April 4. Retrieved from https://advance-lexis-com.ez.lib.jjay.cuny.edu/api/document?collection=news&id=urn:contentItem:5JHS-HJF1-DYNS-314K-00000-00&context=1516831 on July 3, 2020.

McIntosh, E. (2018). Airbnb rentals used for human trafficking, Toronto police say. *The Star*. Retrieved from https://www.thestar.com/news/crime/2018/02/22/airbnb-rentals-used-for-human-trafficking-toronto-police-say.html

Merlan, A. (2020). Here are the most common Airbnb scams worldwide. *Vice*, January 31. Retrieved from https://www.vice.com/en_us/article/epgvm7/airbnb-scam-how-to-tell on July 4, 2020.

Morgan, R. E., & Oudekerk, B. A. (2018). Criminal Victimization. *Bureau of Justice Statistics*. Retrieved from https://www.bjs.gov/index.cfm?ty=pbdetail&iid=6686 on July 2, 2020.

Moyer, & Hsu, 2018 Man used Airbnb sites to stash marijuana in door-to-door delivery operation authorities say. *Washington Post.* Retrieved from https://www.washingtonpost.com/local/public-safety/man-used-airbnb-sites-to-stash-marijuana-in-door-to-door-delivery-operation-authorities-contend/2018/11/02/5e0166ba-deb6-11e8-8c8c-0ba13dcb935a_story.html

Newton, J. (2015). 'Living and dying on Airbnb': Son opens up about father's death at rental home after he was killed on a rope swing by a falling branch. *MAILONLINE*, November 10. Retrieved from https://www.dailymail.co.uk/news/article-3311574/Father-killed-Airbnb-rental-falling-branch-struck-head-sitting-rope-swing-suspended-tree-garden.html on July 3, 2020.

Nyheter, D. (2016). Stockholm prostitutes use Airbnb to set up makeshift brothels. *Worldcrunch*. Retrieved from https://worldcrunch.com/blog/stockholm-prostitutes-use-airbnb-to-set-up-makeshift-brothels

O'Connell, O. (2020). Security guard sentenced to prison for murdering U.S. woman in Costa Rica Airbnb. *Independent*, February 18. Retrieved from https://www.independent.co.uk/news/world/americas/carla-stefaniak-airbnb-costa-rica-murder-bismarck-martinez-security-guard-a9342781.html on July 3, 2020.

Plautz, J. (2015). NYC politician goes undercover at Airbnb listings in illegal hotel sting. *Mashable,* May 1. Retrieved from https://mashable.com/2015/05/01/airbnb-sting-new-york-city/ on July 4, 2020.

Rivas, A. (2019) Airbnb couple finds hidden cameras in bathroom, bedroom: Lawsuit. *NBC San Diego*. Retrieved from https://www.nbcsandiego.com/news/local/airbnb-guests-find-hidden-cameras-in-bathroom-bedroom-lawsuit/2109603/

Rosario, et al. (2014) Airbnb renter returns to 'overweight orgy.' *New York Post.* https://nypost.com/2014/03/17/airbnb-renter-claims-he-returned-home-to-an-orgy/

Sauchelli, D., & Golding, B. (2014). Hookers turning Airbnb apartments into brothels. *New York Post*, April 14. Retrieved from https://nypost.com/2014/04/14/hookers-using-airbnb-to-use-apartments-for-sex-sessions/ on July 4, 2020.

Schneiderman, E. (2014). Airbnb in the City. *New York State Office of the Attorney General.* Retrieved from https://ag.ny.gov/pdfs/AIRBNB%20REPORT.pdf

Seth, A. (2017). Ontario family shocked to discover Airbnb renters using basement to distribute drugs. *Global News*, https://globalnews.ca/news/3843222/ontario-family-shocked-to-discover-airbnb-renters-using-basement-to-distribute-drugs/

Specia, M., & Mzezewa, T. (2019). Adventurous. Alone. Attacked. *The New York Times*, March 25. Retrieved from https://www.nytimes.com/2019/03/25/travel/solo-female-travel.html on July 4, 2020.

Stone, Z. (2016). Living and dying on Airbnb. *Medium*, November 9. Retrieved from https://medium.com/matter/living-and-dying-on-airbnb-6bff8d600c04 on July 3, 2020.

Susko, J., & Schrader, M. (2016). Porn industry uses Airbnb, rental houses for filming. *NBC Los Angeles*. Retrieved from https://www.nbclosangeles.com/news/local/porn-industry-uses-airbnb-rental-houses-for-filming/2086679/

Syfret, W. (2017) Melbourne hosts have allegedly murdered a guest. *Vice.com*. Retrieved from https://www.vice.com/en_uk/article/bj7jmd/melbourne-airbnb-hosts-allegedly-murdered-a-guest

Thomas-Wilson, S., & Lim, J. (2019) Airbnb drug lab bust lands two in court. *The Advertiser*. Retrieved from https://www.pressreader.com/australia/the-advertiser/20190521/281754155783232

Tikader, A. (2020). Airbnb guests cause £4,000 worth of damages. *International Business Times*. Retrieved from https://www.ibtimes.co.uk/airbnb-guests-cause-4000-worth-damages-1676853

Vadaj, R. (2020) Homicide investigation underway after 25-year-old man shot dead at his own birthday party by nephew in Cleveland. *WBTV*. Retrieved from https://www.wbtv.com/2020/04/26/homicide-investigation-underway-after-year-old-man-shot-dead-his-own-birthday-party-by-nephew-cleveland/

Villasanta, A. (2019). Airbnb scam: Users charged for fake bookings, hacked accounts deleted. *International Business Times*. Retrieved from https://www.ibtimes.com/airbnb-scam-users-charged-fake-bookings-hacked-accounts-deleted-2793311

Wiśniewska, A. (2019) Are Airbnb investors destroying Europe's cultural capitals? *Financial Times*. Retrieved from https://www.ft.com/content/2fe06a7c-cb2a-11e9-af46-b09e8bfe60c0

Xu, Y. H., Kim, J. W., & Pennington-Gray, L. (2017). Explore the spatial relationship between Airbnb rental and crime. *Proceedings from Travel and Tourism Research Association: Advancing Tourism Research Globally*. Retrieved from https://scholarworks.umass.edu/cgi/viewcontent.cgi?article=2075&context=ttra on July 3, 2020.

Yaffe, N. (2019). Human trafficking training required for hotels/motels in California by year end. *Fox Rothschild*. Retrieved from https://californiaemploymentlaw.foxrothschild.com/2019/06/articles/advice-counseling/human-trafficking-training-required-for-hotels-motels-in-california-by-year-end/

Yuhas, A. (2015). Airbnb hosts return to find home trashed after 'drug-induced orgy. *The Guardian*. Retrieved from https://www.theguardian.com/technology/2015/apr/30/airbnb-calgary-home-trashed-drug-induced-orgy

Chapter 4
Who Has Legal Responsibility for Safety and Security in Hotels Versus Home Sharing?

Hotels are held to a very high standard when it comes to guest safety and security. These responsibilities have been in place for a significant amount of time in the Western world as they are based on centuries-old British common law known as Innkeeper Laws. These legal expectations focus on the relationship between hotels and guests. In fact, under Innkeeper Laws, hotels generally have more affirmative responsibilities toward their guests than individuals have toward each other under common tort law (Rosendahl 2017). Yet, these rules apply to hotels but not home-sharing companies and hosts, which is likely counterintuitive to guests who take Innkeeper Laws for granted.

The History of Innkeeper Laws The laws relating to the safety and security of innkeepers and their guests in the Western world date as far back as the Middle Ages. These early legal responsibilities provide the foundation for the safety and security expectations relevant to hotels in the United States (Feickert et al. 2006). John E. H. Sherry (1993), in his treatise on the laws of innkeepers, notes that Medieval travel was challenging both because roads were poor and because travelers were regularly beset by outlaws and robbers. As it was not safe to sleep out of doors, nor convenient to carry food, places of business to provide food and lodging arose to meet travelers' needs. Thus, early English common law placed a responsibility on innkeepers to provide safety to guests and their property, and perhaps their horses, and to prevent robbers from entering the premises. Breach of this responsibility could lead to liability.

Further, most of these early inns did not provide individuals with private rooms, but rather the guests slept in large common rooms. As a result, innkeepers also had a legal duty to protect guests during the night from dangers that could arise from strange bedfellows. If an innkeeper provided a guest with a private room with a key, liability for the guest's safety and security shifted slightly. Innkeepers were still responsible for protecting the guest from outside hazards but providing security

C. A. Binns, R. J. Kempf, *Safety and Security in Hotels and Home Sharing*, SpringerBriefs in Criminology, https://doi.org/10.1007/978-3-030-59306-3_4

from other guests was no longer their concern (Sherry 1993). Many of these Medieval rules apply to the hotel sector today.

Modern Innkeeper Laws Today, the responsibility for safety and security of guests and their property lies on the hotel, and safety and security has expanded beyond protecting an individual and their property. The traditional role has expanded from simple guarding and loss prevention (of property of both the guest and innkeeper) to protecting the health and safety of guests from issues as widespread as safe premises to fire to terrorism (Gill et al. 2002). In fact, this responsibility is considered an essential part of the hospitality service's focus on risk management in order to minimize guests' dissatisfaction during their stay (Chauhan et al. 2018; Lisante 1972). Much of these responsibilities have developed over time through litigation, which resulted in court cases that direct the behavior that should protect a hotel from liability. What is required to trigger these responsibilities is a formal relationship between the hotel and guest, where the hotel provides access to their premises to the guest in exchange for money. This means that a traveler cannot make themselves a guest and demand services without the innkeeper's consent and will otherwise be considered a trespasser (Sherry 1993). Further, hotels may refuse a guest if that guest is under the influence and behaving poorly, has a contagious illness, or is pursuing an illegal activity, based on its responsibility to protect other guests (Fox 2019; Law Offices of Stimmel, Stimmel, and Roeser n.d.). The following review is not intended to be exhaustive, but to give the reader an idea of the legal duties placed on hotels regarding safety and security.

A Hotel's Obligation to Protect Guests' Personal Safety and Security A hotel owes guests a right to privacy in their own rooms, which has been declared by the United States Supreme Court as a constitutional right (*Stoner v. California* (1964)). Although this right is currently in a bit of flux since the 2017 Las Vegas incident in which a man shot at concertgoers from a hotel room, killing 59 people including himself, it has long been recognized that there are appropriate safety and security exceptions under which hotel staff have the right to enter a guest's room. Examples include fire or gas leak, misconduct of a guest that offends other guests, or damage to the innkeeper's property (Sherry 1993). Another exception may be to provide emergency medical care to a guest in their room.

Outside of providing privacy, except in emergency situations, a hotel owes a duty to guests to take reasonable care to protect their safety. More specifically, "the standard of care is the care which a reasonably prudent person would exercise under the circumstances" (Sherry 1993, 220). Liability arises only in the case of the hotel's negligence in carrying out this duty. In many jurisdictions, this duty extends to a guest's visitors, both of a personal and business nature. Hotels cannot delegate this responsibility in an effort to avoid liability, and this duty extends outside the inn to areas under the innkeeper's control, such as the parking lot, which should be in good condition, clearly painted, and with adequate lighting (Sherry 1993). Further, a hotel must protect guests from third parties, which could be the innkeeper's employees, other guests, strangers, or intruders (Sherry 1993). In the context of litigation, courts have looked at the general practices of similar sized hotels of a similar quality to determine what measures are reasonable (See, e.g., *Anderson v. Malloy* (1983)). The level of acceptable safety and security measures varies in relationship to the cost charged (Enz 2009; Saied 1990).

A Hotel's Obligations to Protect Guests' Money and Baggage A long-standing line of case law establishes the duty of hotels to receive a guest's baggage along with the person, assuming that the items do not include something dangerous to other guests or the premises (Lord Escher in *Robins v. Gray* (1895)). In most jurisdictions, hotels are responsible for the loss or damage of guests' property, even in cases where there was no negligence on the hotel's part, subject to statutory limitations (Sherry 1993). Typically, statutes limiting the liability of an innkeeper for a guest's property also require a safe or safe deposit box be made available for the guest to protect their valuables.

4.1 Other Legal and Regulatory Responsibilities Placed on Hotels

In addition to Innkeeper Laws, hotels are subject to a plethora of laws and regulations related to safety and security that are established on the federal, state, and local levels. Topics range from ensuring hotel staff do not discriminate on the basis of race, color, religion, sex, national origin, and disability, e.g., according to the Civil Rights Act of 1964 and the Americans with Disabilities Act of 1990 (ADA), to providing heating, lighting, well-maintained premises, and clean and habitable rooms. On top of the legal requirements are the best practices developed by practitioners. Rules related to fire and terrorism, two important issues of safety and security, are detailed more below.

Hotel Obligations Regarding Fire Obligations placed on hotels specifically regarding fire safety can be found in the federal Hotel and Motel Fire Safety Act of 1989. Under this law, hotels who wish to solicit business from federal employees traveling for work must comply with the minimum safety standards of the act, including installing room sprinkler systems and smoke detectors (P.L. 101-391 (1990) as amended by P.L 105-85 (1997); Sherry 1993). Other requirements include "central annunciator panels; guest evacuation sound system; firefighters' voice communication system; smoke-proof, pressurized exit stairs; and an emergency generator for alarm systems, lighting, and smoke exhaust" (US Department of Homeland Security 2010, 7). There are exemptions for establishments with less than four floors or less than six rooms; however, some courts have pointed to these fire standards as "reasonable care," and hotels providing less have been deemed negligent in their duty to provide safety for guests (see, e.g., *Northern Lights Motel, Inc. v. Sweaney* (Alaska 1977)).

Hotel Obligations Regarding Terrorism One authoritative, although not legally binding, set of safety and security standards for hotels regarding terrorism has been promulgated by the US Department of Homeland Security (2010). The standards, drafted in collaboration with the American Hotel and Lodging Association, were developed to address this modern concern. Standards address both accidents and man-made hazards, including improvised explosive devices, chemical or biological attack, vehicle- or aircraft-borne attack, cyberattack, and small arms assault. After performing a risk assessment at the individual property level to determine applicable risks, hotels should develop incident response protocols, including training personnel and establishing communication channels. Additionally, they should establish monitoring, surveillance, and inspection processes. Physical systems employed in a hotel should include: "security systems, … closed-circuit television (CCTV), access control, and electronic key card readers)," which track guest and staff movement (US Department of Homeland Security 2010, 7).

4.2 A Hotel's Protections from Guests' Behavior

The responsibility in the hotel-guest relationship is not one sided. Rather, guests have legal responsibilities toward a hotel they stay in, and failing that, hotels have the right to take action against such guests. For example, hotels have the right to eject a guest or refuse entry to a prospective patron based on improper conduct or objectionable character. This right is based on a hotel's responsibility to safeguard *other* guests and their property. What exactly amounts to improper conduct or objectionable character is an issue to be defined in the course of litigation, but generally, courts apply a reasonableness standard, for instance, whether the hotel's determination reasonable under the circumstances (Sherry 1993). If the determination is deemed reasonable, the individual is considered subject to charges of criminal trespass if they refuse to vacate the premises.

Hotels may also take action in the case of nonpayment: This authority has long been granted innkeepers under the law. In the nineteenth century, innkeepers were authorized to demand payment in advance (*Rex v. Ivens* (K.B. 1920)), but today it is standard practice for a hotel to request a credit card in advance of the stay to which payment can be applied. Guests who overstay the contracted number of days can also be evicted. In many jurisdictions, such as New York, the misdemeanor crime of theft of services can be charged against guests who obtain hotel accommodations through the use of fraud, such as using a stolen credit card or trying to sneak out (New York Penal Law § 165:15 (1978)).

Finally, if a guest damages hotel property, the hotel has several legal remedies. Depending on the jurisdiction, the hotel can charge for damages according to the terms of the hospitality contract, take a guest to court for compensation related to fixing the damages, or request the guest apply to their homeowner's insurance for the costs. Hotels also maintain their own property insurance for these situations as well as other hazards.

4.3 Laws on Safety and Security in Home Shares

Given that the hotel sector is subject to significant laws, regulations, and professional standards, members of the public are not likely to be aware that their rights, responsibilities, and remedies attached to a hotel stay do not apply in the home-sharing setting. Home sharing is considered wholly different from hotels, even though guests receive the same basic services in both settings. In home sharing, the users, both guests and hosts, are solely responsible for their own safety and security.

Section 230 of the Federal Communications Decency Act In contrast to hotels, home-sharing companies, such as Airbnb, VRBO and the like, are shielded from liability under the federal Communications Decency Act of 1986, section 230 (47 USC § 230). This act, which was enacted in 1996, was originally intended to protect people from harassment by others through the use of telecommunications devices, especially including the Internet (Congressional Research Service 1995). Section 230 specifically speaks to companies who create platforms on the Internet that connect members of the public. Such "interactive computer services" are shielded from liability for the activities of the public on such platforms. In other words, it ensures that a company will not be liable for otherwise illegal comments or activities that occur on its Internet platform by individuals for whom the company has no control. Specifically, the statute states: "No provider or user of an *interactive computer service* shall be treated as the publisher or speaker of any information provided by another information content provider" (47 USC § 230, *emphasis added*).

The Federal Trade Commission (FTC), the agency tasked with implementing and enforcing this law, took the stance that this liability shield encouraged entrepreneurship, Internet innovation, and free speech (McNamara 2014). Thus, the FTC advocated for a broad interpretation of the law, especially as regards the definition of "interactive computer service." Courts have followed suit and in repeated instances of litigation have upheld the shield of liability to protect eBay, Craig's List, and Uber, among other similar Internet platform companies supporting elements of the gig economy.

Internet platform companies are also shielded from liability by state and local laws. As discussed, section 230 protects internet platform companies from prosecution under federal law. State and local laws also may not contravene the liability shield under the following language: "No cause of action may be brought and no liability may be imposed under any state or local law that is inconsistent with this section" (47 USC § 230 (e)(1)(3)).

Gentry v. eBay Although appellate courts have not directly ruled on the applicability of section 230 to a home-sharing company, a test articulated by the court in *Gentry v. eBay, Inc.* (Cal. Ct. App. 2002) suggests Airbnb would be shielded from liability under the Communications and Decency Act. In that case, plaintiffs sued eBay charging that the company violated California law when it handled the sale of baseballs and other sports memorabilia with forged signatures and fake certificates of authenticity. The plaintiffs argued eBay had liability as both as a facilitator of the sale and as the provider of false advertising. Regarding the claim of false advertising, plaintiffs pointed to the fact that eBay provided the description of the merchandise, endorsed the seller as a "Power Seller," and, as part of its service, provided a feedback forum for buyers' comments.

The court was not swayed by the plaintiffs' arguments. It noted that the service eBay provided was to connect buyers and sellers and not to make sales itself. It simply made sellers' descriptions available to potential buyers. Further, they determined the designation of "Power Seller" was derived from a calculation of the proportion of positive comments in the feedback forum that a seller received, not from any assessment made by eBay itself. Finally, the feedback forum was simply an accountability mechanism for buyers to help sellers be accountable for their wares and services. Just because eBay provided the forum for users did not make eBay liable for activity on that forum that was inaccurate or slanderous. As such, eBay was protected from the claims of liability the plaintiffs had brought.

The similarities between the court's description of eBay in *Gentry v. eBay* and the home-sharing model are striking (McNamara 2014). For example, Airbnb makes descriptions of home-sharing properties available to potential guests, but these descriptions are written by the hosts themselves. It also has a mechanism to identify "Superhosts," who are those who have received a high proportion of good reviews from guests. Finally, Airbnb provides a forum on its website where guests can rank hosts, their properties, and services. (Likewise, hosts can rank guests.) One may conclude that section 230 would completely shield Airbnb from liability as it did eBay in *Gentry v. eBay.*

Unsuccessfully Suing Airbnb Over a Guest's Safety and Security An example of a suit against Airbnb in which Airbnb was shielded from liability can be found in a case filed in a California district court in the summer of 2017, when Leslie Lapayowker made headlines for what was touted as the first lawsuit against Airbnb (Levin 2017; Vora 2017). Lapayowker, a home-sharing guest, sued both the host, Carlos Del Olmo, and Airbnb. She alleged that Del Olmo sexually assaulted her and that Airbnb breached its fiduciary duty to her as a consumer and provided false and misleading advertising. Further, she claimed Airbnb was negligent in labeling the host as "verified" and a "superhost" – labels she relied on when making her booking (*Lapayowker v. Airbnb,* et al., Complaint (2017)).

In the petition to the San Francisco County Superior Court, Lapayowker stated that Del Olmo took multiple actions to make her uncomfortable during her stay. For example, he made sexually suggestive comments to her, pounded on her windshield while she sat in her car, and used drugs in front of his underage son. This behavior drove her to leave the month-long booking after only 3 days. She reported that when she returned a week later to retrieve some of her belongings, which she had left behind, Del Olmo invited her inside, locked the door, and forcibly kissed her while masturbating (*Lapayowker v. Airbnb,* et al., Complaint (2017)).

Regarding Airbnb, Lapayowker argued that Airbnb acts as a real estate broker rather than a simple internet platform (*Lapayowker v. Airbnb,* et al., Complaint

(2017)). The petition argued that Airbnb's actions to advise lessors/hosts about how to effectively let their place and improve their profits, including describing the property and offering professional photography services to advertise properties, gives rise to a duty to guests who rely on Airbnb's information. In particular, the plaintiff pointed to the "verified identification" and "superhost" labels as misleading.

"Verified identification" is a tool that Airbnb promotes as its background check process (Airbnb 2013). When a user's identification is verified, it means Airbnb's tool has matched the user's online name provided to Airbnb, LinkedIn, or Facebook with a scanned photo ID or other personal historical information. This name-matching was the extent of the background check Airbnb provided at the time. This was important in Lapayowker's case, because it was learned Del Olmo had a criminal record, which could not have been identified with this type of background check.

"Superhost" is a term that Airbnb uses to "celebrate and reward its top-rated and most experienced hosts" (Airbnb 2020). According to the Airbnb website, a superhost is a host who has: (1) a rating of 4.8 or above from a minimum of 50% of their guests in the last year; (2) hosted 10 or more stays in a year, or 100 nights over three guest's stays; (3) zero cancellations; and (4) a 90% response rate to guest questions. Airbnb identifies superhosts with a badge on their profile, provides these hosts a 20% bonus for referring new hosts to Airbnb, and advertises that superhosts earn up to 22% more than other hosts.

After reporting the assault to law enforcement and Airbnb, Lapayowker learned that Del Olmo had been arrested in a domestic violence case in Florida for which he entered a diversion program (Levin 2017). She questioned the accuracy of Airbnb's assertion that it runs background checks on all United States hosts and guests. She suggested that Del Olmo should have never been allowed to serve as a host. Airbnb responded by removing Del Olmos from the website, but stood by its assertion that they had completed their background check done for each host and user (Vora 2017).

Six months after the petition was filed, court documents show that the claims against Airbnb were quietly dismissed with prejudice (*Lapayowker v. Airbnb*, et al., Request for Dismissal, (2017)). Thus, Airbnb escaped all liability for the harm done toward this guest. Only the case against the host Del Olmos has continued.

4.4 Local Attempts to Regulate Home Sharing

Despite section 230, some cities and states have tried to regulate the home-sharing market by imposing requirements on home-sharing hosts, or if the hosts are renters, on the landlords who own the property. These municipalities argue that they are not regulating home-sharing companies, but rather the use of the property within their jurisdiction. Cities to have done so include New York City, San Francisco, Miami, Denver, Los Angeles, New Orleans,[1] and states of New York, New Jersey, Indiana,

[1] Cities across the world have also moved to regulate Airbnb. To see a comparison of five European

and Massachusetts. As an example of these efforts, this section closely examines the activities in the city and state of New York.

Both New York City (NYC) and New York State (NYS) depend on tourism to support their economies. Tourism Economics, an international organization that analyzes travel data, quantified state's 2018 tourism service as follows:[2]

- Number of tourists: Approximately 253 million, with 65.1 million visiting NYC alone (McGeehan 2019)
- Economic Impact: $114.8 billion, including $71.8 billion in direct spending
- State and local taxes generated: $8.9 billion
- Employment: 957,800 jobs, with 291,084 employed in NYC alone (Center for an Urban Future 2018)

As a result of this reliance, both on the state and local levels, policymakers have had some unease about the presence of home-sharing diminishing hotel tax collections and local employment. Further, in NYC, concerns have been raised about Airbnb hosts reducing the availability of housing options for residents and itinerant guests threatening the safety and security of permanent residents. Three primary regulatory approaches have been used to address concerns about home sharing in NYC and NYS, in particular focusing on Airbnb, as follows:

- Regulating hosts offering illegal home-sharing properties
- Imposing consequences on landlords who own the property being used for illegal home sharing
- Requesting data on home-sharing listing directly from Airbnb

These approaches have had spotty success, leaving issues of safety and security primarily in the hands of users.

Regulating Hosts Offering Illegal Home-Sharing Properties The New York legislature has taken steps to regulate home sharing in both *private dwellings*, defined as dwellings with one or two families living independently (New York (NY) Multiple Dwellings Law (Mult. D) § 4(6)), and *multiple dwellings*, defined as dwellings with three or more families living independently (NY Mult. D § 4(7));[3] however, different restrictions apply to these two settings. These regulatory steps are the most closely connected to issues of health and safety.

For private dwellings, NYC's zoning authority applies. Building codes or fire codes must be met before transient guests may stay in the home. Depending on the location of the home, the host may have to apply for exemptions to zoning restrictions and/or be subject to inspections of their property. Failure to do so has resulted

---

and six American cities' home-sharing regulations, see Nieuwland and van Melik (2018).

[2] Statistics are from Cuomo (2019) unless noted otherwise.

[3] In NYC, private dwellings are located primarily in the boroughs of Brooklyn, Queens, and Staten Island, whereas multiple dwellings are primarily located in Manhattan and the Bronx.

in problems to home-sharing hosts, which have been reported by local news outlets. Examples follow.

- A resident in the neighborhood of Bedford-Stuyvesant in Brooklyn reported that although she had researched the legality of offering part of her single-family home for home sharing, she was surprised to be fined for multiple violations related to the safety and security of her home, amounting to nearly $5000 (Real Deal Staff 2019).
- Another homeowner in Brooklyn found herself facing $10,000 in fines for her two unit townhome based on alleged fire code violations. She has appealed the decision based on her assertion that the inspectors had not entered her home before they assessed her penalties (Chamoff 2019).

For multiple dwellings, so called "*class A multiple dwellings*," i.e., apartment buildings, are distinguished from "*class B multiple dwellings*," which are abodes for transient guests, i.e., hotels (NY Mult D § 9). By law, apartment buildings (class A multiple dwellings) may *only* be used for permanent residence purposes, defined as "occupancy of a dwelling unit by the same natural person or family for thirty consecutive days" (NY Mult D § 4(8)(a)). Specifically prohibited are paying guests who stay for less than 30 days when the permanent occupants are away for personal reasons, such as vacation or medical treatment (NY Mult D § 4(8)(a)(1)(B)). In other words, home sharing without the host on location is prohibited. One who does so can be charged with a misdemeanor (NY Mult D § 304), and one who advertises home sharing that does n't meet statutory requirements can be fined as much as $7500 (NY Mult D § 121). Further, rent stabilization rules may apply. Tenants in rent-stabilized apartments may not make a profit on their below-market apartments.

Based on these state statutes, New York City has taken steps to enforce these laws when they have been violated by hosts who are tenants of apartment buildings or owners of condominiums in Class A multiple dwellings. Efforts were enhanced in April 2019 when Mayor Bill DeBlasio increased the budget of the city's Office of Special Enforcement and tasked the office to specifically examine illegal home sharing (New York City Office of Special Enforcement 2020; Goldensohn 2017). The following are examples of steps the City has taken against would-be hosts in Class A multiple dwellings

- In November 2018, the NYC Office of Enforcement made headlines when it issued over 20 violations to condominium owners in a single high rise building on Manhattan's Far West Side. The enforcement was called "one of the largest yet" by a real estate trade paper (Real Deal Staff 2018) The individuals cited were found to be regularly renting out their properties through Airbnb inconsistently with state laws, which neighbors had repeatedly complained about.
- In February 2019, NYC sued multiple defendants for conspiring to act as independent Airbnb hosts using more than 100 host accounts. The defendants, who had created 18 separate corporations to support this endeavor, rented apartments and then turned around and offered these properties on Airbnb even though none of the defendants ever lived there. The City alleges that these hosts earned $20 million illegally (Ferré-Sadurní 2019).

Imposing Consequences on Landlords Based on NYS laws, NYC has fined landlords for allowing illegal home sharing to go on their properties.

- The case listed above from February 2019 was exposed because NYC fined at least one building owner for illegal home sharing, who turned around and sued the renters/hosts to recover the cost of the fines that were assessed based on the renters' actions. The extent of the scam was then made public (Ferré-Sadurní 2019).
- In December 2019, the NYC Office of Special Enforcement sued 10 individuals, primarily members of a single family, who owned four walk-up multiple dwellings in the East Village, Manhattan. The family had reported multiple vacancies in the buildings, but investigators found that these units were being rented by a limited liability company who advertised these properties on Airbnb. A second tenant of multiple units did the same. These actions not only violated laws against home sharing, but contravened laws regarding rent stabilization. It was estimated that the hosts illegally earned over $2.2 million over 3 years (NYC Office of Special Enforcement 2019).

Requesting Data on Home-Sharing Listings Directly from Airbnb The state and city of New York have both taken steps to demand information from Airbnb about the listings within NYC, with limited success. In 2014, then Attorney General Eric Schneiderman released a report that suggested nearly 75% of the Airbnb listings in NYC were illegal (Streitfeld 2014a). It also appeared that certain single units were booked repeatedly (as many as 13 times on average per night, suggesting it was used as a brothel) (Schneiderman 2014).

Based on this evidence, and under his authority to investigate illegal acts, specifically violations of the Multiple Dwelling Law and established hotel occupancy taxes, Schneiderman subpoenaed Airbnb's records of all NYS hosts, their addresses, rates charged, dates of guests' stays, method of payment, and total gross revenue. Airbnb filed suit to quash the subpoena for being overbroad, and the state court agreed with Airbnb (*Airbnb, Inc. v Schneiderman*, (N.Y. Sup. Ct. 2014)). The court stated the information that the Attorney General requested was not closely tied to the alleged illegal acts identified in his initial report, largely because the scope was the entire state, not just NYC, but also because some of the information requested was not directly relevant to the alleged illegal acts.

Subsequently, Airbnb and the Attorney General were able to compromise. Airbnb agreed to provide the information asked for, but anonymized. All names and personally identifiable information were not to be provided. Furthermore, Airbnb agreed to provide information to hosts in NYS about the Multiple Dwelling Law as well as other legal requirements they face (Streitfeld 2014b).

A few years later, NYC moved forward with a strategy similar to that initially pursued by the Attorney General, and with similar results. In 2018, the City Council passed a bill that would require any home-sharing platforms, including Airbnb, to disclose on a monthly basis hosts' names and listing addresses to the City's Office of Special Enforcement (Ferré-Sadurní 2018; Greenberg 2018). The legislation included a $1500 fine per listing that home-sharing companies failed to provide. Immediately, Airbnb filed for an injunction against the law in the federal courts, arguing that this law amounted to an illegal search and seizure without probable cause, violating the 4th Amendment of the US Constitution. The federal judge again agreed with Airbnb and struck down the law (Weiser and Goodman 2019). Currently, Airbnb, along with other home-sharing companies, and the city's Office of Special Enforcement are negotiating a resolution that serves both parties (Dolmetsch and Carville 2020).

4.5 What Legal Options Are Available to Guests and Hosts to Do If They Are Wronged in a Home-Sharing Situation?

Currently, the options are limited to two: (1) purchasing insurance to help prevent issues and (2) bringing actions in court.

Insurance Perhaps unsurprisingly, insurance companies have created new products to cover unexpected issues arising specifically from home sharing. For hosts, short-term rental insurance is touted to fill gaps that might exist in a homeowner's insurance policy. This extra coverage generally comes in the form of a rider or endorsement on an existing policy or as a replacement for a host's homeowner's policy. The product should cover damage and/or loss of a host's real and personal property as well as costs relating to a personal injury sustained by a guest. It can also cover typical business liabilities and loss of business income.

For guests, special travel insurance is available. Typical travel insurance covers emergency medical issues, emergency travel needs, and trip cancellation costs. Insurance specific to home sharing can cover rearranging travel plans and finding a new place to stay if the host's home is not safe and secure or otherwise acceptable.

Law Suits Private causes of action based on traditional property, tort, and contract law are available to both guests and hosts (Marzen et al. 2017). This cause of action will be dependent on the particular facts of the case, but one might sue on the basis of premises liability, nuisance, right to privacy, or property damage or loss, for some examples. In certain cases, landlord-tenant law may apply (Rosendahl 2017).

Some legal scholars have argued that private legal action is sufficient to deal with the issues that might arise between host and guest (see, e.g., Briggs 2018; Marzen et al. 2017). These arguments are made to support that position that neither regulation nor the imposition of traditional innkeeper laws on the peer relationships created in home sharing is necessary. Yet, this remedy is in fact limited, because there are economic and other barriers to bringing a lawsuit, including hiring a lawyer and gaining access to court (Rhode 2001).

An alternative argument has been made that because the lines between the host-guest and the landlord-tenant relationships have been blurred, a new regulatory scheme is necessary (Rosendahl 2017). It is said that the obligations imposed on landlords and tenants are too onerous for individuals not in the business of being a landlord, and likewise, the traditional responsibilities imposed on innkeepers would harm the home-sharing economy. As such, uniform regulation at the federal level could solve the problem by imposing rules that are right-sized for home-sharing hosts and guests. The endorsement of this approach by Congress remains to be seen.

4.6 Conclusion

Several issues are made clear by a review of the legal rules applicable to home sharing. First, the state of the law is unsettled in regard to guests' and users' safety and security. Arguably neither the traditional Innkeeper laws and those applicable to landlords and tenants are quite appropriate. Local jurisdictions are scrambling to figure out how to fill the gap. Second, and perhaps more important, home-sharing companies benefit from a unique status of being liability proof. Thus, the safety and security of both guests and hosts are in their own hands. The next chapter builds on this understanding of the legal framework by closely examining the typical safety and security practices occurring in hotels and home shares.

Works Cited

Airbnb. (2013). Airbnb announces "Verified identification." *Airbnb.com*. Retrieved from https://www.airbnb.com/press/news/airbnb-announces-verified-identification on June 15, 2020.

Airbnb. (2020). Superhost terms and conditions. *Airbnb.com*. Retrieved from https://www.airbnb.com/superhost/terms on June 15, 2020.

Airbnb, Inc. v Schneiderman, 989 N.Y.S.2d 786, 44 Misc. 3d 351, 2014 N.Y. Misc. LEXIS 2270 (N.Y. Sup. Ct. 2014).

Americans with Disabilities Act of 1990, Pub. L. No. 101-336, § 2, 104 Stat. 328 (1991).

Anderson v. Malloy, 700 F.2d 1208 (8th Cir. 1983).

Briggs, K. (2018). The new blame game: How Airbnb has been mis-regulated as the scapegoat for century-old problems. *Business Entrepreneurship & Tax Law Review, 2*, 155–177.

Center for an Urban Future. (2018). Destination New York. *NYCFuture.org*. Retrieved from https://nycfuture.org/pdf/Destination_NY.pdf on July 6, 2020.

Chamoff, L. (2019). New York City townhouse owners are being fined thousands for illegal Airbnbs. *Forbes*. Retrieved from https://www.forbes.com/sites/lisachamoff/2019/12/26/new-york-city-townhouse-owners-are-being-fined-thousands-for-illegal-airbnbs/#29eef8ae47df on July 6, 2020.

Chauhan, A., Shukla, A., & Negi, P. (2018). Safety and security measures adopted by the hotels and their impact on customer management. *International Journal of Research, 6*(1), 118–125.

Civil Rights Act, 42 USCS sec. 2000e (1964).

Communications Decency Act of 1986, as amended in 1995, section 230 (47 USC § 230).

Congressional Research Service. (1995, February 1). *Summary: S.314*. Communications Decency Act of 1995. Retrieved from https://www.congress.gov/bill/104th-congress/senate-bill/314/ on July 6, 2020.

Cuomo, A. M. (2019). *Governor Cuomo announces record breaking numbers for great New York state fair attendance and statewide tourism*. Retrieved from https://www.governor.ny.gov/news/governor-cuomo-announces-record-breaking-numbers-great-new-york-state-fair-attendance-and on July 4, 2020.

Dolmetsch, C., & Carville, O. (2020, March 3). NYC sues Airbnb software partner in escalation of feud. *Bloomberg*. Retrieved from https://www.bloomberg.com/news/articles/2020-03-02/new-york-city-extends-war-on-airbnb-by-targeting-guesty on July 6, 2020.

Enz, C. A. (2009). The physical safety and security features of U.S. hotels. *Cornell Hospitality Quarterly, 50*(4), 553–560. https://doi.org/10.1177/1938965509345 96.

Feickert, J., Verma, R., Plaschka, G., & Dev, C. S. (2006). Safeguarding your customers. *Cornell Hotel and Restaurant Administration Quarterly, 47*(3), 224–244. https://doi.org/10.1177/0010880406288872.

Ferré-Sadurní, L. (2018, June 26). To curb illegal Airbnbs, New York City wants to collect data on hosts. *New York Times*. Retrieved from https://www.nytimes.com/2018/06/26/nyregion/illegal-airbnb-new-york-city-bill.html?searchResultPosition=1 on July 3, 2020.

Ferré-Sadurní, L. (2019, February 23). Inside the rise and fall of a multimillion-dollar Airbnb scheme. *New York Times*. Retrieved from https://www.nytimes.com/2019/02/23/nyregion/airbnb-nyc-law.html on July 3, 2020.

Fox, J. T. (2019, January 1). What hotels need to know about their legal obligations. *Hotel Management*. Retrieved from https://www.hotelmanagement.net/legal/legal-obligations-hoteliers on July 6, 2020.

Gentry v. eBay, Inc., 121 Cal. Rptr. 2d 703 (Cal. Ct. App. 2002).

Gill, M., Moon, C., Seaman, P., & Turbin, V. (2002). Security management and crime in hotels. *International Journal of Contemporary Hospitality Management, 14*(2), 58–64. https://doi.org/10.1108/09596110210419237.

Goldensohn, R. (2017, April 26). De Blasio ramps up Airbnb enforcement. *Crain's New York Business*. Retrieved from https://www.crainsnewyork.com/article/20170426/REAL_ESTATE/170429915/mayor-bill-de-blasio-budgets-1-6-million-to-crack-down-on-airbnb on July 6, 2020.

Greenberg, Z. (2018). New York City looks to crack down on Airbnb amid housing crisis. *New York Times*. Retrieved from https://www.nytimes.com/2018/07/18/nyregion/new-york-city-airbnb-crackdown.html?searchResultPosition=5 on June 11, 2020.

Hotel and Motel Fire Safety Act of 1989, Pub. L. No.101 (1990) as amended by P.L. 105-85 (1997).

Lapayowker v. Airbnb, et al. (2017). Complaint, San Francisco County Superior Court, CGC-17-560425 (July 27).

Lapayowker v. Airbnb, et al. (2017). Request for Dismissal, San Francisco County Superior Court, CGC-17-560425 (December 20).

Law Offices of Stimmel, Stimmel and Roeser. (n.d.). *The law and liability of hotels*. Retrieved from https://www.stimmel-law.com/en/articles/law-and-liability-hotels on July 6, 2020.

Levin, S. (2017, July 27). Airbnb sued by woman who says she was sexually assaulted by 'superhost'. *The Guardian*. Retrieved from https://www.theguardian.com/technology/2017/jul/27/airbnb-guest-sexual-assault-allegation on July 6, 2020.

Lisante, T. W. (1972). Improving hotel security. *The Cornell H.R. Quarterly, 13*(1), 2–10.

Lord Escher, M. R., in *Robins v. Gray* (1895), 2 QB 501 (1895).

Marzen, C., Prum, D. A., & Alberts, R. J. (2017). The new sharing economy: The role of property, tort, and contract law for managing the Airbnb model. *New York University Journal of Law and Business, 13*(2), 295–336.

McGeehan, P. (2019, August 19). N.Y.C. is on pace to draw a record 67 million tourists this year. *New York Times*. Retrieved from: https://www.nytimes.com/2019/08/19/nyregion/nyc-tourism.html?auth=login-email&login=email on July 6, 2020.

McNamara, B. (2014). Airbnb: A not-so-safe resting place. *Colorado Technology Law Journal, 13*(1), 149–170.

New York City Office of Special Enforcement. (2019). *Office of Special Enforcement sues to stop displacement of rent-stabilized units in four east village buildings*. Retrieved from https://www1.nyc.gov/site/specialenforcement/news/sues-to-stop-displacement-of-rent-stabilized-units-2019-12-16.page on 6/11/2020.

New York City Office of Special Enforcement. (2020). *Enforcement*. Retrieved from https://www1.nyc.gov/site/specialenforcement/enforcement/enforcement.page on June 11, 2020.

New York CLS Multiple Dwellings Law.

New York Penal Law, § 165:15 (McKinney Supp. 1978).

Nieuwland, S., & van Melik, R. (2018). Regulating Airbnb: How cities deal with perceived negative externalities of short-term rentals. *Current Issues in Tourism, 22*(7), 811–824. https://doi.org/10.1080/13683500.2018.1504899.

Northern Lights Motel, Inc. v. Sweaney, 561 P.2d 1176, rehearing, 563 P.2d 256 (Alaska 1977).

Real Deal Staff. (2018, November 12). City officials conduct one of the largest Airbnb raids at far west side condo building. *The Real Deal*. Retrieved from https://therealdeal.com/2018/11/12/city-officials-conduct-one-of-the-largest-airbnb-raids-at-far-west-side-condo-building/ on June 11, 2020.

Real Deal Staff. (2019, April 5). Small homeowners are facing hefty fines for short-term rentals. *The Real Deal*. Retrieved from https://therealdeal.com/2019/04/05/small-homeowners-are-facing-hefty-fines-for-short-term-rentals/ on June 11, 2020.

Rex v. Ivens, 7 Car. and P. 213, 173 Eng. Rep. 667 (K.B. 1920).

Rhode, D. L. (2001). Access to justice. *Fordham Law Review, 69*(5), 1785–1820.

Rosendahl, M. (2017). iTenant: How the law should treat rental relationships in the sharing economy. *William and Mary Law Review, 59*, 731–770.

Saied, J. (1990). Approaches to risk management. *Cornell Hotel and Restaurant Administration Quarterly, 31*(2), 45–55.

Schneiderman, E. (2014). *Airbnb in the city*. New York State Office of the Attorney General. Retrieved from https://ag.ny.gov/pdfs/AIRBNB%20REPORT.pdf on July 6, 2020.

Sherry, J. E. H. (1993). *The laws of innkeepers: For hotels, motels, restaurants, and clubs*. Ithaca: Cornell University Press.

Stoner v. California, 376 United States 483 (1964).

Streitfeld, D. (2014a). Airbnb listings mostly illegal, New York state contends. *New York Times*. Retrieved from https://www.nytimes.com/2014/10/16/business/airbnb-listings-mostly-illegal-state-contends.html on June 11, 2020.

Streitfeld, D. (2014b). Airbnb will hand over host data to New York. *New York Times*. Retrieved from https://www.nytimes.com/2014/05/22/technology/airbnb-will-hand-over-host-data-to-new-york.html?searchResultPosition=8 on July 6, 2020.

United States Department of Homeland Security. (2010). *Protective measures guide for the U.S. lodging industry*. Retrieved from https://info.publicintelligence.net/DHS-HotelProtection.pdf on June 4, 2020.

Vora, S. (2017). Airbnb sued by guest who says a host sexually assaulted her. *New York Times*. Retrieved from https://www.nytimes.com/2017/08/02/travel/airbnb-lawsuit-host-sexual-assault.html on July 6, 2020.

Weiser, B., & Goodman, J. D. (2019). Judge blocks New York City law aimed at curbing Airbnb rentals. *New York Times*. Retrieved from https://www.nytimes.com/2019/01/03/nyregion/nyc-airbnb-rentals.html?searchResultPosition=8

Chapter 5
What Are the Contemporary Safety and Security Practices Used in Hotels and Home Shares?

For hotels, safety and security has always been important. The traditional hotel detective, stereotypically depicted in classic Hollywood movies such as *The Maltese Falcon*, is evidence of the hotel service's long-standing, visible attempts to address issues related to dishonest employees, dishonest guests, and dishonest members of the public pursuing crimes like theft or prostitution (Lisante 1972). This approach to security, i.e., preventing illegal activities of individuals, has over time expanded to loss prevention and the health and safety of employees and guests (Groenenboom and Jones 2003). This broader approach helps address the vulnerabilities that arise from the fact that hotels offer 24–7 services, attract a wide range of people, and are open to the public. These safety and security measures are designed to protect hotel guests and their property, employees and their possessions, hotel visitors, as well as the hotel itself (Lisante 1972).

Still, regardless of whether one stays in a hotel or in a home share, concerns about safety and security arise. Everyone that travels takes certain risks – becoming a potential victim of a crime and having one's safety compromised are among those risks. The problem that has been illustrated in many examples throughout this work is that certain crimes can more easily occur in a private home let through the home-sharing process as opposed to in a hotel. These cases suggest that if these guests had stayed in hotels, they would have been less likely to experience such negative outcomes. The examples further demonstrate that home-sharing hosts take a risk that their home could be the scene of a crime/an accident and that home-sharing guests are vulnerable with regard to the safety and security of their bodies and property.

Some of these risks and vulnerabilities will be discussed here, coupled with the safety and security practices employed by hotels and home shares. Ultimately, this chapter highlights how many steps are taken in hotels to keep people safe and secure as compared to home shares. It also explores who, in the absence of these practices, is responsible for safety and security in the home-sharing setting. To do so, the safety and security practices of hotels compared to home shares will be reviewed.

C. A. Binns, R. J. Kempf, *Safety and Security in Hotels and Home Sharing*, SpringerBriefs in Criminology, https://doi.org/10.1007/978-3-030-59306-3_5

Then, the safety and security guidance that is provided to its users by Airbnb will be examined. Finally, this chapter sets forth the apparent security and safety responsibilities of all parties.

5.1 Safety and Security Concerns and Measures Taken to Address Them

Guests' safety and security concerns are no different when sleeping at a hotel versus sleeping in a home share; however, hotel workers and owners are in the full-time profession of hospitality, while most home-sharing hosts are not. Hotels are also legally obligated to provide many safety and security features that home shares are not. Education on safety and security is difficult to disseminate in the home-sharing setting because hosts are extraordinarily decentralized, as is typical of the gig economy. As a result, the safety and security practices in the two settings are very different.

Table 5.1 compares the safety and security practices typically used by hotels on one hand and users of Airbnb (both hosts and guests) on the other. Here Airbnb is again an exemplar for home-sharing companies. These practices address a wide variety of safety and security concerns. The table is sorted into types of concerns: those related to the room; the building; the surrounding area; the employees; and other unique considerations. The table shows stark differences between the responses voluntarily taken and/or mandated by law for hotels versus home-sharing hosts (specifically Airbnb hosts).[1]

As evidenced in Table 5.1, safety and security practices are far more robust in hotels as opposed to home shares. The safety and security features provided are commensurate with their hotels' legal obligations under statutes, regulations, or legal case law, and the hotels are inspected to confirm compliance. For home shares, most of these features are suggested but not required, and inspections of hosts' homes are not conducted.

5.2 What Guidance Does Airbnb Provide to Its Users Regarding Safety and Security?

Home-sharing companies are not legally obligated to make sure safety or security features are available, but it is not clear if users understand that the companies are also not responsible for incidents in a home share. That said, even without legal

[1] A fuller discussion of the laws and regulations relative to safety and security in both settings is found in Chap. 4.

Table 5.1 Safety and security concerns and practices taken to address them by hotels and Airbnb hosts

Safety/security concern	Preventative measure	Are hotels required to provide?	Are Airbnb hosts required to provide?
Safety and security issues related to the room			
Carbon monoxide poisoning	Install carbon monoxide detector	In some states	No, but suggested by Airbnb
Emergencies requiring evacuation	Emergency action routes/instructions/ directions	Yes	No, but suggested by Airbnb
Fire	Fire/smoke detector	Yes	No, but suggested by Airbnb
Fire	Fire sprinklers	Yes	No, but suggested by Airbnb
Poor room hygiene	Maintain room cleanliness	Yes	No, although Airbnb asks hosts to refrain from listing uninhabitable spaces
Room security	Install locks/deadbolts/ night latch on door	Yes	No
Room security	Provide electronic keys to track entry	No, but recommended	No
Unsafe drinking water	Ensure water hygiene	Yes	No, although Airbnb asks hosts to disclose if water is unavailable
Unsafe or inaccessible for physically disabled guests	Provide Americans with Disability Act (ADA) compliant rooms	Yes	No, although Airbnb allows hosts to advertise if their properties are ADA compliant
Safety and security concerns related to the building			
Alerts to miscellaneous emergencies	Emergency systems (fire alarms and security alarms)	Yes	No
Cyberattacks	IT security	Yes	No, although for its own website, Airbnb has established several security procedures
Detection of other miscellaneous emergencies	Hazard detectors in various areas of hotel	Yes	No
Emergencies requiring evacuation	Emergency plans and procedures	Yes	No, but suggested by Airbnb
Fire	Fire extinguishers available	Yes	No, but suggested by Airbnb
Heart-related medical emergencies	AED defibrillator units	Yes	No
Lack of legal authorization to provide hospitality	Establish that the location is legally authorized to be used for hospitality	Yes	No, although Airbnb strongly suggests that hosts only post legal listings

(continued)

Table 5.1 (continued)

Safety/security concern	Preventative measure	Are hotels required to provide?	Are Airbnb hosts required to provide?
Loss of power	Emergency power source (generators)	Yes	No, although Airbnb asks hosts to disclose if electricity is unavailable
Medical emergency	First aid kits	Yes	No
Other electrical problems	Electrical safety preparedness	Yes	No, although Airbnb asks hosts to refrain from listing uninhabitable spaces
Safety of facilities and guests	Security guards or other security personnel	Yes	No, but may already be present for some listings
Safety and security concerns related to the surrounding area			
Building security	Building can be locked and kept secure	Yes	No
Natural disasters	Natural disaster preparedness	Yes	No
Other risks arising from the surrounding area	Risk assessments for property and surrounding areas	Yes	No
Safety and security concerns related to employees and guests			
Employees abusing drugs	Drug testing	Possibly, at the discretion of the hotel	No
Employees abusing their authority	Background checks conducted	Yes	No
Employee verification	Employee photo IDs	Yes	No
Guests using false identities	ID verification of guests by staff	Yes	No, but hosts may ask for ID at check-in
Human trafficking and other illegal acts pursued by guests	Specialized training to identify human trafficking, prostitution, terrorism, etc.	Yes	No
Staff assistance in emergencies	Emergency situation training	Yes	No
Other safety and security concerns			
Guests' lack of knowledge of safety and security hazards	Provide guest awareness for possible hazards	Yes	No, but suggested by Airbnb
Lack of protection for female guests and solo travelers	Special precautions for these guests	No, but recommended	No, but some hosts may have features more suitable for female guests or solo travelers
Slow response from local law enforcement	Develop relationships with the local law enforcement	No, but recommended	No, but some hosts may have connections to local law enforcement
Unexpected costs and damage protection	Liability insurance	Yes	Yes

Sources: Airbnb (2020a), National Conference of State Legislatures (2018), Nondiscrimination on the Basis of Disability (2020) and U.S. Department of Homeland Security (2010)

responsibility, home-sharing companies provide some guidance about safety and security protocols to help users have good experiences.

Using Airbnb as an example, the company provides education to users and has imposed some rules, such as prohibiting party houses after a deadly incident in California at a Halloween party in 2019 where multiple people were shot. Yet, what is made evident is that even with the modicum of protections provided by Airbnb, including offering free smoke and carbon monoxide detectors to hosts, users' security and safety is primarily left in their own hands, whether host or guest, especially as compared to hotels.

Airbnb states on its website: "Your safety is our priority … On any given night, 2 million people stay in homes on Airbnb in 100,000 cities all over the world. There are more than 6 million listings in 191 countries to choose from – that's more than the top five hotel chains combined. What makes all of that possible? Trust" (Airbnb 2020j). To help build this trust, Airbnb states that it provides several services on its platform: secure communication and payment systems on its website, two-way reviews, background checks, managing the relationship between hosts and guests, and focusing on communication between users and with Airbnb itself.

The Airbnb website is used to connect hosts and guests as well as transfer payment from the guest to the host, with fees paid to Airbnb for their service. Airbnb states that if hosts and guests interact solely on their website, security issues should not be a problem, because they use a multistage verification process before people can sign in. Further, they send email notifications upon any change made in a user's account, including logins from new locations (Airbnb 2020j). These steps are crucial to an online platform that handles money, but a quick search of "Airbnb" and "hacking" on Google results in multiple users, usually guests complaining that their accounts were hacked with strangers making reservations using their credit card on file and then changing passwords to block the original user from entering the account. Sometimes, it is suggested that these reservations were to fake listings. These anecdotal reports suggest that there may be security issues related directly to the Airbnb platform, a fate not uncommon for any online business, but for which Airbnb is shielded from liability.

Two-way reviews are Airbnb's method to provide some transparency about host-guest interactions. Both hosts and guests review each other on the Airbnb website after the guest's stay with the host. The idea is that future guests and hosts will have some information about their potential hosts and guests, respectively, which will help them make a safe decision. This only works to the extent that people are honest with their reviews. Airbnb's review policy requires reviews to be unbiased and relevant. Further, the policy states that positive reviews may not be incentivized or obtained by threats (Airbnb 2020c). Nevertheless, this type of policy is hard to police. Airbnb relies on complaints about reviews to trigger its action and will deactivate accounts if there are repeated violations but also takes the position that it "does not mediate disputes concerning truth or fairness" (Airbnb 2020c).

Background checks are used to augment the two-way reviews. Airbnb also provides its own assessment of guests and hosts, albeit the review is not as stringent as one might like. Guests and hosts are "verified," in that Airbnb confirms guests' identities by comparing the individual's legal name, address, and picture ID with a current photo and evidence of address. Background checks for those in the US also include a check against "regulatory, terrorist, and sanction's watchlists" (Airbnb 2020g). Airbnb does offer a caveat for this process, stating on its website: "Completing this process isn't an endorsement of any host or guest, a guarantee of someone's identity, or an assurance that interacting with them will be safe. Always use your own best judgment, and follow our safety tips for guests and hosts" (Airbnb 2020g).

For guests' information specifically, Airbnb designates some hosts as meeting "Airbnb plus" standards. In these cases, a host's property is evaluated by an in-person visit to ensure the property is well-maintained, clean, has good water pressure and working appliances, and provides fully equipped kitchens and amenities such as filtered or bottled water (Airbnb 2020h). Bedrooms in shared spaces are also verified to have working locks. Further, some hosts are identified as "SuperHosts." These are hosts who are in good standing due to meeting specific performance standards: at least ten reservations or three reservations of over 100 days each quarter, at least 90% response rate, no more than a 1% cancellation rate, and having at least a 4.8 rating out of five. It should be noted that, in all caps, Airbnb specifies in the legal terms of the Superhost program that "Airbnb does not endorse any Superhost nor guarantee or control the quality, safety, suitability, or conduct of any host, regardless of whether or not a host is a Superhost." (Airbnb 2020i).

For the hosts' information, Airbnb explains that "every Airbnb reservation is scored for risk and we cancel any bookings that appear suspicious" (Airbnb 2020f). There is little information on the Airbnb website that explains this risk scoring. The only statement is that it is "using predictive analytics and machine learning to instantly evaluate hundreds of criteria to identify suspicious activity before it happens" (Airbnb 2020j).

Airbnb further *shapes the relationship between the host and guest* in setting some global rules that apply to all stays and by allowing hosts to control how they want to do business. Some rules include limitations on large parties, a prohibition on open invite parties, and prohibitions on discrimination. Hosts are encouraged to set their own house rules, such as whether guests can smoke, bring pets, or have parties. Airbnb gives hosts the authority to cancel reservations of guests who violate the house rules (Airbnb 2020f). Hosts may also demand from guests a government-issued ID, a verified phone number, positive reviews from other Airbnb hosts, and personal communication. Airbnb explains that if a guest makes a host feel unsafe, they can refuse a reservation. If they feel unsafe after they have accepted a reservation, they can cancel the reservation, but may be required to pay a penalty for that cancellation if house rules were not broken.

To protect their property, hosts can charge a cleaning fee and/or ask for a security deposit. Airbnb not only strongly recommends that hosts also secure appropriate insurance to protect their property and remove valuables from the property but also makes available what they call the "Airbnb Host Guarantee." This guarantee is not insurance but can provide up to $1 million for damages to the property that meet the Airbnb guidelines for the program (Airbnb 2020b). Also, Airbnb provides "Host

Protection Insurance," which can be used if a host is sued by a third party for the third party's bodily injury or property damage (Airbnb 2020e).

Finally, Airbnb focuses on *communication with users*. The company encourages hosts to learn about how to make their homes accessible to individuals with disabilities. Also, it provides safety workshops to hosts and touts 24–7 worldwide support in 11 languages (Airbnb 2020j). Last but not least, Airbnb offers some safety recommendations on their website, detailed further in Table 5.2. This table shows that hosts and guests both have responsibilities for the safety and security of property and people. Hosts have primary responsibility for the presence of safety and security features, while guests are responsible for making sure their home share has the safety and security features that are important to them.

All the approaches listed in Tables 5.1 and 5.2 can help users be safe and secure while staying in a home share, but it is really important to remember that if one's safety and security is threatened, home-sharing companies will not be liable for any problems. These companies can rely on federal law if things go wrong, and as a result, guests and hosts are legally responsible for issues that arise during a home-sharing stay.

Yet, a home-sharing company can be more encouraging than simply recommending and/or educating. Airbnb, for example, asks hosts on their website to institute various protocols as a part of responsible hosting practices and report the features they employ on their listings. Therefore, the host not only has the decision whether to comply but also has incentive to be able to advertise to guests the steps they have taken. Airbnb takes the same approach with their higher tier properties. In the Airbnb Plus program, hosts are "required" to confirm they have smoke and carbon monoxide alarms as a condition of the program, which allows the host's property to get preferential attention on the Airbnb website.

Notably, there are limitations in this approach. Although Airbnb will provide fire alarms or carbon monoxide detectors free of charge to hosts, it does not guarantee the equipment will arrive;[2] however, the hosts are responsible for requesting them, installing them on their property, making sure they are in good working order, and noting these features on their listings. In Airbnb's "terms and conditions" for receiving a free smoke detector, Airbnb tells hosts, "you remain entirely and solely responsible for your listing, including but not limited to its safety equipment and condition" (Airbnb 2020d). Airbnb will not confirm the presence of these features. Similarly, in the Airbnb Plus program, the obligation is on the host to act, and again, their word is accepted as confirmation, as Airbnb doesn't require any confirmation or proof of installation (Airbnb 2018). Unfortunately, as noted in Chap. 3, hosts do not always implement safety features in their properties (Kennedy et al. 2019).

There are also multiple safety and security concerns not addressed in Airbnb's educational materials. For example, the website does not address natural disaster

---

[2] In their "terms and conditions" for receiving a free smoke detector, Airbnb tells hosts, "You are responsible for complying with any regulations or limitations on courier, postal service providers, personal shipments, and/or personal imports that may apply to you or your territory" (Airbnb 2020d).

Table 5.2 Safety practices recommended by Airbnb of hosts and guests

Safety practice	Description of safety practice recommended by Airbnb	Host's role	Guest's obligation
Carbon monoxide detector	Detector is installed in the hallway of the home near sleeping areas. Detector is tested once a month.	Install carbon monoxide detector. A host can request a single detector from Airbnb, provided at no charge.	Ask the host if they have a carbon monoxide alarm installed. Guests should consider bringing their own, portable model to home shares, regardless.
Emergency plan	Plan includes two ways to escape from every room in the listed property, contact information for local emergency services, and a meeting spot at a safe distance from the home for guests to reconnect after a fire.	Establish a written emergency plan.	Ask the host for a copy of the emergency plan.
First aid and CPR training	First aid and CPR training courses are completed.	Sign up for and complete first aid and CPR training.	Ask hosts if they are trained in first aid and CPR and request to see proof of completion – especially if the guests doesn't have this training themselves.
First aid kit	A first aid kit is available, and guests are made aware of it.	Have a first aid kit available in a location made obvious to guests.	Ask about the presence of the first aid kit and confirm its location and contents upon arrival.
Habitable spaces	Shared spaces are habitable, without "substandard cleanliness or undisclosed lack of running electricity or water."	Provide habitable spaces for guests. Any basic features that are not available are disclosed in the listing.	Ask the host to confirm the presence of basic services – especially if the listing seems ambiguous in this regard. Guests should also check the water and electricity status immediately upon entering their rental unit.
Other hazards	Make guests aware of any potential hazards.	Identify potential hazards and notify guests.	Ask hosts if there are any potential hazards in the home, property, or surrounding area they should be aware of. Consider performing independent research about the property and the surrounding community for the presence of any potential hazards.

(continued)

Table 5.2 (continued)

Safety practice	Description of safety practice recommended by Airbnb	Host's role	Guest's obligation
Professionally installed appliances	Appliances are installed according to manufacturer's instructions and local building codes by professionals.	Have appliances installed by professionals.	Exercise caution when using appliances, as the installation practices cannot be easily confirmed.
Secure payment transactions	Business is to be transacted only through the Airbnb payment system. Users are asked not to "commit booking fraud, credit card fraud, or launder money; divert payments meant for others."	Transact business only inside the Airbnb payment system.	Exercise caution and never transact with a host outside of the Airbnb platform for any reason.
Smoke alarms	Alarms are installed at every level of the home and outside each sleeping area. Alarms are tested once a month, and batteries are replaced at least once a year.	Install smoke alarms. A host can request a single smoke alarm from Airbnb, provided at no charge.	Ask the host if they have smoke alarms installed and whether they are in good working order.

Source: Airbnb (2020a)

preparedness or safety and security risk assessments. Also, hosts are also not trained to identify criminal acts like human trafficking, prostitution, or terrorism, nor is any training recommended. There are no special requirements for solo travelers or "at risk" travelers.

There is also a lack of discussion about door and key security. There are inherent security concerns when hosts provide keys to home-sharing guests. In hotels, their keys are controlled to prevent misuse. Oftentimes, they are electronic and cannot be copied. However, in a private home, these controls are not in place. When a host shares a key to their house or apartment with multiple short-term guests, security problems have resulted. Residents of one building in Australia shared their experience with this to the *Docklands News*. Their Airbnb nightmare began when their amenities, such as the swimming pool, gym, sauna, and spa, were damaged by an influx of Airbnb guests. To combat this issue, the building decided to limit entry to residents only. This upset Airbnb guests, who physically and verbally retaliated against the building security personnel. Building security key fobs were found to have been copied and sold on Ebay. At least one guest burglarized an apartment, due to their ability to gain unauthorized access. All of this resulted in increased security and maintenance costs for residents, who had to pay to repair the damages and to upgrade the security key fobs (March 2020).

5.3 Based on Contemporary Practices, How Does a Guest Decide Whether to Stay in a Hotel or a Home Share?

This review of safety and security practices suggests guests should do a cost-benefit analysis of sorts. From a safety and security perspective, what is the guest's comfort with the uncertainty that comes with a home share? How does that uncertainty balance against staying at a unique location that most likely costs less? How important is the comfort of a hotel? Is it worth the extra price?

The answer to this type of cost-benefit analysis will depend on the individual, but research suggests that many guests will choose a hotel because it provides greater safety and security. Hotel guests in the U.S. have stated that it's worth the extra cost for the heightened safety and security measures that hotels offer (Enz 2009). A survey of 930 US hotel guests found they were "willing to pay 10 percent above the regular nightly rate to cover the security features they would accept" (Feickert et al. 2006, p. 234). These studies suggest that many guests, if they can afford it, prefer the safety and security hotels provide. Thus, not only are safety and security features desired by guests, but also they can be profitable for hotels. Nevertheless, considerations for hotel guests and home-sharing guests and hosts are reviewed below.

The next sections present things to consider about staying in a hotel versus home share.

Considerations Regarding Hotels As Table 5.1 makes clear, hotels, in contrast to home shares, have a legal obligation to provide a certain level of protection to their guests, and that obligation is reflected in their robust safety and security features. Hotels will likely pay more but will be assured they will have the tools they need to be safe and secure and their personal obligation is minimal.

That said, a minimal obligation is not a zero obligation. Guests should familiarize themselves with the provided safety and security tools and information and be ready to act if needed. They should learn what to do in the event of an emergency, including knowing the evacuation plan, usually located behind the door of each hotel room (Bowers 2014). They should also review the building's exterior for the general layout of fire exits and escapes (an escape diagram is located at each elevator). If guests are familiar with their closest emergency exits, an evacuation in the case of emergency can be a lot more efficient, which could save lives.

Guests learned the importance of their role at a Philadelphia Sheraton hotel in 2014. There, reports of smoke in the basement caused them to evacuate the 757 room hotel. Because the hotel had a comprehensive safety program, staff were certainly prepared for the evacuation; however, a lack of guest awareness was said to have impacted the response time. According to the Executive Philadelphia Fire Chief, it took the guests 90 min – a time he considered "dangerously long" yet "quite common" due to an average guest's general lack of familiarity with safety procedures (Bowers 2014). He told the public, "It is up to you as a hotel guest to be responsible for knowing the floor diagram, the evacuation procedure and where the exits are located" (Bowers 2014).

In addition to threats to a guest's safety from issues like fire, hotel guests are known to be targets for local criminals (Lisante 1972). As a result, guests should take basic security measures. They should be familiar with common crimes. Most thefts from hotel rooms involve jewelry or money (Lisante 1972). Guests who secure these items in their provided safe and make sure their door is always locked are less likely to experience a loss (Lisante 1972). Also, hotel guests should be aware of their surroundings, because due to the public nature of a hotel's "private" property, hotel staff can have challenges providing security. Large hotels are like a "city within a city," and thousands of people can be present in a hotel at any given time. Many hotel crimes are opportunistic and can be prevented by guests who exercise vigilance (Lisante 1972).

Interestingly, scholars have proposed that too much security presence and messaging in a hotel can lend guests to think crime won't occur (Groenenboom and Jones 2003). If they feel completely secure, they will drop their guard. Obvious security may also invite criminals who may want to take on the challenge (Groenenboom and Jones 2003). For these and other reasons, hotel security managers have said it is challenging to ensure both "maximum security" and "high hospitality standards" in the hotel setting (Groenenboom and Jones 2003).

Considerations Regarding Home Sharing If a guest determines that home sharing is preferable, they need to understand that they bear the greatest security risk and burden. They are especially vulnerable. They are sleeping away from home, in someone else's territory, and must exercise a heightened sense of vigilance. They cannot rely on background checks, the presence of safety and security features, or compliance inspections. For that reason, home-sharing guests need to take an extremely proactive approach to their safety and security. They cannot assume that hosts will provide what they need, and they can't assume that the home-sharing company will be responsible for any negative outcome.

That said, it is also important to note that safety and security risks in home sharing are constantly evolving. Often when a problem occurs, new policies and practices are constantly being instituted. Critics have negatively described Airbnb's approach to security highly reactionary (Stone 2016), but the resulting response can lead to better safety and security for all users.

One example is Airbnb's rule to prohibit unauthorized open parties in home shares, which was created in response to a deadly incident in California. In November 2019, an Airbnb was rented in Orinda, which is located 15 miles east of San Francisco. The guest lied to the host, saying they needed the rental on Halloween to escape the smoke from neighboring wildfires (Durbin 2019). In reality, their intent was to host a Halloween party. News of this party was posted on Instagram, and it drew over 100 attendees. Police were called to the property following noise complaints. On route to the scene, the officers learned gunfire was also reported. Then, upon arrival, the officers found a "highly chaotic scene that included gunshot victims, injured partygoers, and numerous people fleeing the scene." Five people died due to the violence that occurred at this party. Two firearms were recovered from the scene. In this case, the host was properly registered with the City as a home share, and 13 people were legally permitted on the property. However, the property had been subject to previous complaints from neighbors for large parties and trash. With over 100 guests at this property, this party was clearly in violation of City ordinances. Following this event, Airbnb banned "party houses" and vowed to "get rid of abusive host and guest conduct," even though prior to November 2019, these parties were known to occur all over the country (Durbin 2019). Airbnb created a "rapid response team" for house parties and announced plans to expand screening for "high risk" reservations. Hopefully, these changes result in a safer environment for many communities.

Another incident that led Airbnb making a policy change was an instance of carbon monoxide poisoning in December, 2013. At that time, six women were staying in an Airbnb apartment in Taiwan for a wedding. Tragedy occurred when one guest was found dead and her friends so ill they needed hospitalization (Stone 2016). Later, it was reported that a leaking water heater located in an enclosed balcony next to the home share filled the home with carbon monoxide (Stone 2016). The property was found to be an illegal home share, which was run by two men who didn't have permits, didn't have carbon monoxide detectors, and didn't conform to "structural or fire safety standards" (Stone 2016). Immediately following this incident, Airbnb started offering free carbon monoxide detectors to hosts who request them (Stone 2016).

Tips for Home-Sharing Guests Ideally, guests should be aware of safety and security issues from before they book a home share until they vacate their home share. There are many steps that may be taken in this regard. A nonexhaustive list is presented here. Before booking, guests should consider:

- Educating themselves about potential safety and security risks
- Understanding the types of things that can reduce these risks
- Reviewing the safety and security advice of the home-sharing company
- Assessing the disclosures of potential hosts, considering what is disclosed and what is not
- Researching local regulations to make sure home sharing is permitted
- Researching crime data of the local area

For the stay, guests should consider:

- Purchasing travel insurance that specifically includes home shares
- Purchasing and bringing a portable carbon monoxide detector
- Bringing Clorox wipes or other cleaning supplies to address cleanliness concerns

When arriving at the home share, guests should consider:

- Asking the host to review their emergency plan
- Verifying the location of security alarms, fire alarms, or other hazard detectors.

Finally, during the stay, guests should remain aware of their surroundings inside and outside the home share.

Tips for Home-Sharing Hosts The primary step for hosts is to implement the safety and security practices that are appropriate for their home. A secondary step is to purchase insurance relevant to home sharing. Depending on the home-sharing company, needs may vary.

Out of the 33 safety and security features described in Table 5.1, the primary safety/security feature Airbnb provides to hosts is liability insurance. In January 2015, Airbnb started providing $1 million in host protection insurance. The insurance covers harm that occurs to guests and/or the guests' property. This was an important addition for Airbnb on behalf of their users, given most insurance companies will not cover "business use" of a property, which includes home-sharing rentals (Howard 2015; Lieber 2014). At first, Airbnb offered this insurance as secondary coverage, which was helpful in areas such as San Francisco, where hosts are required to have a minimum of $500 k liability coverage on their home shares (Lieber 2014). In 2015, Airbnb made this insurance, which is free, primary coverage (Lieber 2015).

Still hosts should not assume that they don't need to worry about their coverage. Other home-sharing companies may not offer insurance or provide coverage to address all possible cases and damage (Uprety 2016). Also, home-sharing companies can change what they provide. For example, Home Away only started offering its liability insurance in 2017 (May 2017). Even though Airbnb provides primary coverage to hosts, the company advises hosts to check with their insurer and consider purchasing their own additional coverage to fill any potential policy loopholes (Lieber 2015). For example, a policy might not cover the damage to a host's property not caused by the guest (Uprety 2016). Another policy might cover commercial use, but many don't.

Hosts should not think potential incidents are too "rare" to cause concern. Unfortunately, rare incidents happen in home rentals. In one case, in 2019, a couple from North Dakota staying in a home share property in San Diego died after a tree randomly fell on the house, killing them as they slept (Bravo 2019). This incident was described as "very rare" by the local police lieutenant (Bravo 2019). In that case, it was said the burden was on the homeowner to maintain the trees on their property, although liability could shift if the incident was deemed to happen due to weather (Bravo 2019). It is unknown how the insurance company settled the matter. Nevertheless, this case demonstrated a unique issue where the liability was somewhat ambiguous, and the host would have been wise to have contacted their insurance company in advance of booking the guest, just to be sure.

For Zak Stone, whose father died while using an outdoor swing at their Airbnb in Texas (see Chap. 3), it was the host's homeowner's insurance that covered the claim. Stone suggested that they were "lucky" the host's insurance company didn't "deny coverage for commercial activity" (Howard 2015).

5.4 Conclusion

This chapter shows that typical safety and security practices in hotels vary greatly from those in home shares. Further, when looking at Airbnb, for example, one sees that the company gives some guidance to users about how to protect themselves and their property, but this guidance is not comprehensive or required. As a result, guests and hosts who pursue home sharing need to understand that the weight of safety and security falls on their shoulders. The next chapter explores criminological theory to identify how this situation might be improved.

Works Cited

Airbnb. (2018). Airbnb introduces new global measures to help keep people safe. *Airbnb.com*. Retrieved from https://news.airbnb.com/new-safety-measures-2018/ on June 28, 2020.

Airbnb. (2020a). Airbnb. *Airbnb.com*. Retrieved from https://www.airbnb.com/ on July 7, 2020.

Airbnb. (2020b). Airbnb's host guarantee. *Airbnb.com*. Retrieved from https://www.airbnb.com/guarantee on June 15, 2020.

Airbnb. (2020c). Airbnb's review policy. *Airbnb.com*. Retrieved from https://www.airbnb.com/help/article/2673/airbnbs-review-policy on June 12, 2020.

Airbnb. (2020d). Home safety terms and conditions. *Airbnb.com*. Retrieved from https://www.airbnb.com/help/article/1128/home-safety-terms-and-conditions on July 8, 2020.

Airbnb. (2020e). Host protection insurance. *Airbnb.com*. Retrieved from https://www.airbnb.com/host-protection-insurance on June 15, 2020.

Airbnb. (2020f). How Airbnb protects hosts. *Airbnb.com*. Retrieved from https://www.airbnb.com/d/safety on June 15, 2020.

Airbnb. (2020g). How does it work when Airbnb verifies your identity? *Airbnb.com*. Retrieved from https://www.airbnb.com/help/article/1237/how-does-it-work-when-airbnb-verifies-your-identity on June 12, 2020.

Airbnb. (2020h). Introducing Airbnb plus. *Airbnb.com*. Retrieved from https://www.airbnb.com/plus on June 12, 2020.

Airbnb. (2020i). Superhost terms and conditions. *Airbnb.com*. Retrieved from https://www.airbnb.com/superhost/terms on June 15, 2020.

Airbnb. (2020j). Your safety is our priority. *Airbnb.com*. Retrieved from https://www.airbnb.com/trust on June 12, 2020.

Bowers, M. (2014, July 24). Hotel evacuation safety tips. *NBCPhiladelphia.com*. Retrieved from https://www.nbcphiladelphia.com/news/local/hotel-evacuation-safety-tips/89877/ on July 7, 2020.

Bravo, C. (2019). 2 Dead after massive tree crushes Point Loma Heights home. *7 San Diego*. Retrieved from https://www.nbcsandiego.com/news/local/large-tree-collapses-on-point-loma-heights-home/1861/

Docklands News. (2020, March 2020). "We live here". *Docklands News*. Retrieved from: https://www.docklandsnews.com.au/columns/detail/we-live-here-march-2020_16142/

Durbin, D. A. (2019). Airbnb says it's banning 'party houses' after a shooting at a Halloween party in California killed 5 people. *Business Insider*. Retrieved from https://www.businessinsider.com/airbnb-ceo-says-company-is-banning-party-houses-2019-11

Enz, C. A. (2009). The physical safety and security features of U.S. hotels. *Cornell Hospitality Quarterly, 50*(4), 553–560. https://doi.org/10.1177/193896550934596.

Feickert, J., Verma, R., Plaschka, G., & Dev, C. S. (2006). Safeguarding your customers. *Cornell Hotel and Restaurant Administration Quarterly, 47*(3), 224–244. https://doi.org/10.1177/0010880406288872.

Groenenboom, K., & Jones, P. (2003). Issues of security in hotels. *International Journal of Contemporary Hospitality Management, 15*(1), 14–19.

Howard, A. (2015, November 10). A man died at an Airbnb rental. Here's how the company responded. *Huff Post*. Retrieved from https://www.huffpost.com/entry/a-death-at-an-airbnb-rental-puts-the-tech-company-in-the-hot-seat_n_5640db66e4b0b24aee4b18f7 on July 2, 2020.

Kennedy, H., et al. (2019). Reported fire safety and first-aid amenities in Airbnb venues in 16 American cities. *Injury Prevention, 25*, 328–330.

Lieber, R. (2014, December 5). A liability risk for Airbnb hosts. *New York Times*. Retrieved from https://www.nytimes.com/2014/12/06/your-money/airbnb-offers-homeowner-liability-coverage-but-hosts-still-have-risks.html on July 3, 2020.

Lieber, R. (2015, November 13). Death in Airbnb rental raises liability questions. *New York Times*. Retrieved from https://www.nytimes.com/2015/11/14/your-money/death-in-airbnb-rental-raises-liability-questions.html on July, 2020.

Lisante, T. W. (1972). Improving hotel security. *The Cornell H.R. Quarterly, 13*(1), 2–10.

May, K. (2017, May 16). HomeAway quietly introduces $1 million liability insurance. *Phocus Wire*. Retrieved from https://www.phocuswire.com/HomeAway-quietly-introduces-1-million-liability-insurance on July 7, 2020.

National Conference of State Legislatures. (2018). *Carbon monoxide requirements, laws and regulations*. Retrieved from https://www.ncsl.org/research/environment-and-natural-resources/carbon-monoxide-detectors-state-statutes.aspx on June 4, 2020.

Nondiscrimination on the Basis of Disability by Public Accommodations and in Commercial Facilities, 28 CFR Part 36 (2020).

Stone, Z. (2016, November 9). Living and dying on Airbnb. *Medium*. Retrieved from https://medium.com/matter/living-and-dying-on-airbnb-6bff8d600c04 on July 3, 2020.

United States Department of Homeland Security. (2010). *Protective measures guide for the U.S. lodging industry*. Retrieved from https://info.publicintelligence.net/DHS-HotelProtection.pdf on June 4, 2020.

Uprety, M. (2016). Vacation rental insurance: Which policies protect homeowners? *Lodgify*. Retrieved from https://www.lodgify.com/blog/vacation-rental-insurance/ on July 10, 2020.

Chapter 6
What Does Criminological Theory Suggest About Sleeping Away from Home?

The central thesis of this work focuses on responsibility for safety and security in home shares. Previous chapters have made clear that the responsibilities that were traditionally placed on professional hoteliers have shifted to home-sharing hosts and guests, whereas home-sharing companies have responsibility only to the extent that they choose to take it on. Even then, in the United States, these companies are currently shielded from any legal liability that arises from safety and security problems. This chapter turns to several academic theories, specifically the theories of defensible space, rational choice, and routine activities, to understand why, from a criminological perspective, this policy shift is problematic for both safety and security, but especially for security. These theories are also used to begin to develop recommendations that will be fleshed out in the final chapter of this brief.

6.1 Defensible Space Theory Suggests Buildings and Homes Can Be Designed to Be More Secure, But Residents Must Play a Role in Providing Security

Defensible space is at its base a security design concept (Merry 1981). In 1972, Oscar Newman proposed a "model for residential environments that inhibits crime by creating the physical expression of a social fabric that defends itself" (Newman 1972, p. 3), thereby coining the term "defensible space." The model has four key features: building form, windows, location, and space (Merry 1981; Newman 1972). Each of these features have an important security function. First, a building's form may thoughtfully be designed in such a way as to reduce security vulnerabilities. Second, the strategic placement of windows may provide security by increasing the "natural surveillance" of public areas. Third, the location of the structure may be more or less secure based on its proximity to threatening areas. Finally, the space

C. A. Binns, R. J. Kempf, *Safety and Security in Hotels and Home Sharing*, SpringerBriefs in Criminology, https://doi.org/10.1007/978-3-030-59306-3_6

may be designed to "influence" inhabitants to be territorial and, thus, defend the space (Merry 1981, p. 398–399; Newman 1972, p. 50).

Newman's theory explores how the design of buildings and the selection of their locations intertwine with the contributions of residents toward achieving security goals. For example, using defensible space theory, it has been asserted that the most secure buildings are small, low rise structures (Merry 1981; Newman 1972). Larger buildings are considered a less secure space because their size and breadth make inhabitants unable to monitor the space well. Further, more inhabitants mean that there are more visitors, i.e., strangers, in the space. Inhabitants are less likely to develop a relationship – a sense of "territory" or "community" – with a space that is filled with many strangers. Thus, without this sense of space, this theory suggests residents are less likely to defend their neighborhood (Merry 1981, p. 399; Newman 1972, p. 50).

Newman cited research regarding New York City public housing developments to support his theories. He hypothesized that the largest developments, which included multiple high-rise buildings with large numbers of residents and visitors, would have the highest crime rates (Merry 1981; Newman 1972). Further, he also suggested that the worst security design prototype is "the slab with high-rise banks of apartments on both sides of the corridor serviced by a central elevator" (Merry 1981, p. 399; Newman 1972, p. 50), because this design inhibited the inhabitants from performing natural surveillance of the space.

Since Newman proposed the defensible space theory, other scholars have used his model to help further explain how building structures can increase, or decrease, the likelihood that inhabitants will defend their space. For example, adding "real and symbolic barriers," such as security bollards or tall bushes, or creating "strongly defined areas of influence," achieved by dividing the property into subzones, helps to not only make the inhabitants feel safer but encourages them to protect that sense of security. Also, adding "improved opportunities for surveillance" such as well-placed windows and doors, offer clear lines of sight to observe people and activities (Newman 1972, p. 3; Reynolds and Elffers 2009, p. 29).

It is important, however, to note that defensible space theory suggests that design elements are "a necessary, but not sufficient condition for crime prevention" (Merry 1981, p. 420). Rather, people are crucial to success. In 1981, Sally Merry illustrated this concept in her study of a well-designed but crime-ridden east coast housing development. At first glance, the design of the development suggested security. The housing was low and small, with few points of entry and adequate, well-positioned windows. Yet, the building had high crime rates, and residents lived in fear. Nearly half of the residents interviewed had been a victim of robbery, burglary, or assault since moving into the building. Merry concluded that the residents themselves contributed to the lack of security. In particular, residents hadn't gotten to know their neighbors and, therefore, didn't develop a sense of "territory" or "community." As a result, residents were unable to identify the presence of outsiders and any accompanying security threats.

Thus, defensible space theory suggests that keen environmental design should be supported by strategies that emphasize community cohesion. While structures can be designed to enhance visibility and observability, which increases the chance that potential offenders are caught, residents must make the observations (Reynolds and Elffers 2009). If residents are encouraged to enhance their sense of "territoriality" and "community," they will function as security agents. Their security roles are in turn facilitated by the environmental design (Newman 1972). The two elements interplay.

An example of a successful melding of security concerns with a sense of community is "neighborhood watch" (Rosenbaum 1987). A community with a neighborhood watch program acts as the "'eyes and ears' of the police," reducing crime by increasing the risk of detection and apprehension (Rosenbaum 1987, p. 106). Typically, these programs encourage residents to meet regularly to share information about such things as local crime problems, prevention tips, and detection strategies. A key element behind the success of a neighborhood watch program is that local residents are familiarized with each other, which "encourages intervention [with] and reduces fear" of strangers to the area (Rosenbaum 1987, p. 107). This is helpful for the entire community because fear of crime has been associated with a lower quality of life (Stafford et al. 2007). Further, neighborhood watch programs help participants feel "responsibility and control" over what happens in their community (Greenberg et al. 1982; Rosenbaum 1987; Skogan 1981).

Another example is the US Department of Homeland Security's campaign: "If you see something, say something." This campaign's focus is on communication as a tool to help to foster the open dialogue about security issues, which leads to a sense of shared community. This in turn serves to bring the space "under the control of its residents" (Newman 1972, p. 3).

There are some caveats to defensible space theory. First, while defensible space informs security design, it is not an exact science. Crime rates and environmental design are correlated (Repetto 1976; Pyle 1976; Duffala 1976; Molumby 1976); but overall, researchers are quite vague about the process and determinants of defending space, and much of it remains not well understood (Merry 1981, p. 398). Second, the role of a building's inhabitants cannot be underestimated. Carefully designed defensible spaces are not always defended by their communities. In instances where the spaces were defensible, yet crime occurred, it is thought that the social conditions of the neighborhood inhibited residents from safeguarding their space in some way (Merry 1981; Atlas 1991).

Defensible Space and Hotels Hotels, like multiresident buildings and neighborhoods, also have crime concerns arising from the presence of strangers (or in this case, customers), which they often address using defensible space theory tactics (Huang et al. 1998). From a security perspective, a regular concentration of "strangers" makes it more challenging for locals to determine who belongs in the area (Dong 2017, p. 72); however, hotels, being in the business of hospitality to strangers and often part of a large corporation, generally have the advantage of security experts at their disposal to address these specific concerns (Dong 2017). As such, many tactics consistent with defensible space theory are used in the hotel setting. For instance, many hotels are designed to have only one entrance. This allows for natural surveillance and reduces the risk of crime (Huang et al. 1998). Another example is placing a mirror across from an elevator, which allows guests to observe those who get off the elevator with them. Finally, on-site security teams provide monitoring and surveillance, including proactive measures and immediate response in the event of emergency.

Hotels also incorporate the defensible space concept of "image and milieu" (Huang et al. 1998, p. 83), based on the deliberate creation of a sense of welcoming community. Hotels work hard to prevent any negative images of their properties on the part of guests and, therefore, monitor their property and the surrounding area ensuring that the property is clean and inviting and free of "panhandlers, littering, and graffiti," which has the goal of reducing the risk of victimization (Huang et al. 1998, p. 83). As expected, they have the dedicated ground staff to ensure timely and continuous ground maintenance.

Defensible Space and Home Sharing Like hotels, home sharing caters to largely transient strangers. However, there are critical differences between the two settings. The hotels are specifically designed to welcome and accommodate strangers. These commercial spaces have often been designed with defensible space tactics in mind, including on-site physical security presence, which simply cannot be duplicated in the average residential environment.

In contrast, most private homes do not have the security features present in hotels. Elements including secured access, opportunities for natural surveillance, and other defensive space tactics may not be present or even possible for a host to implement. Apartment buildings and other multiresidential buildings are more likely to have been designed with defensible space tactics in mind, which can be helpful from a security perspective; however, neither apartment buildings nor residential neighborhoods were designed to manage the coming and going of large volumes of transient persons.

According to the defensive space theory, home sharing is disruptive to the provision of security in several ways. First, the home and the community that is being shared is not likely to have incorporated defensible space design tactics, unless a host and/or the community has been educated in security tactics. Second, and perhaps more critically, home sharing interferes with the ability of residents to actively participate in making their area more secure.

According to defensible space theory, security risks are increased when residents don't remain relatively static, because a neighborhood where neighbors are known to one another facilitates security. A stable community allows residents to notice when someone is out of place in their neighborhood. Also, in stable communities, formal and informal community groups can be established to monitor the neighborhood. Critics of home sharing say that communities in popular tourist destinations are losing "neighbors" (Barber 2016). In this sense, home sharing disrupts the ability of residents to recognize their own community members. Also, temporary guests will not be in a position to contribute to community security.

Safety and security concerns are compounded in many areas due to the large volume of short-term rentals. In the United Kingdom, one member of parliament reported in her borough alone that 3600 properties were available on Airbnb (Ellery et al. 2018). The complaints she hears "range from security and fire safety concerns to noise nuisance and rubbish dumping as visitors come and go every couple of days" (Ellery et al. 2018).

Ann Arbor, Michigan, is currently considering a ban on home sharing for this reason. Proponents argue that the multiple properties offered on home-sharing platforms are having a negative impact on the community's security. Residents have painted the situation as dire, stating: "there's not a long-term resident to be found; it's just sort of a rotating line of tourists in and out" (Stanton 2019a). Not only is the ability to conduct surveillance challenged, but other negative consequences arise when guests do not have the same interest in protecting the quality of life in the community. To this end, Ann Arbor residents report multiple safety and security concerns including "transients, parties, illegal activity, parking and safety concerns, garbage, and noise" (Stanton 2019a).

The safety and security issues residents report in Ann Arbor are happening across the globe. Another example comes from residents in Australia who told their story to the local *Docklands News*. There, a resident said that home sharing "took over" their building, with one-third of it comprised of short-term residents. This brought many safety and security concerns to the building. The overall apathy and the absence of care and lack of community among residents made this resident feel "unsafe." Also, the "large groups of noisy guests" caused damage to the building's hallways and elevators. Homeowners' association dues were increased to offset these costs. This homeowner ended up selling their home and moving away at a financial loss, just to avoid this situation (March, 2020).

A similar concern is expressed in areas where the number of parties has proliferated due to home sharing. In fact, some guests are known to pursue home sharing for the sole purpose of having parties. These parties are an apparent source of revenue for the guest, turned host. Residents in Chicago said home-sharing parties in their neighborhood were held as a money making scheme, because people were seen collecting an entry fee at the door (Chavarria 2019). In the UK, party hosts reportedly make "a fortune" (Ellery et al. 2018).

These parties bring unsafe conditions and security hazards to communities. In Ann Arbor, residents reported smelling marijuana smoke, hearing screaming in the early morning hours, and seeing party patrons funneling beer out of residential windows or climbing onto neighboring roofs (Stanton 2019b). These home-sharing parties have been reported in many other cities across the globe, including Dallas, Texas; Chicago, Illinois; Athens, Greece; Barcelona, Spain; Taupo, New Zealand; and Docklands, Australia (Burgen 2020; Docklands News 2020; Spielman 2020; Stanton 2020; Toler 2020; Wiśniewska 2019). In the United Kingdom, residents say these parties have "degraded the quality of life and character of communities" (Ellery et al. 2018).

The so-called "party house" situation became such a problem that Airbnb had to ban them in 2019 (Chavarria 2019). This ban came after several people died at a shooting that took place during a house party in California (see Chap. 5). Although celebrated by many, the ban drew the attention of critics, who think it came too late and should have happened before needless deaths occurred (Chavarria 2019). Some also wonder whether the ban will really have an effect, since there is no obligation of enforcement on the part of the home-sharing service (Durbin 2019).

Such people are not only very unlikely to add any security value to the neighborhood but present a security risk. In fact, there is anecdotal evidence that guests of illegal home shares have been instructed to lie about using Airbnb (Plautz 2015). During the New York City Assembly member's 2015 investigation, she recorded video footage of one host telling her "If somebody asks you something, never mention in the building Airbnb; This is supposed to be residential" (Plautz 2015). In 2019, a reporter in Canada who posed undercover as an Airbnb guest at a condo complex in Toronto was given a set of rules from his host, which said "If anyone asks, you're just visiting; Please don't mention Airbnb or short-term rental. It's prohibited in the condominium building" (Cowley et al. 2019). Then, on check-in day, the host reminded him "Don't mention anything about Airbnb, OK? They don't like it here" (Cowley et al. 2019).

Conclusions About Defensible Space Theory and Home Sharing Defensible space theory suggests that the community needs to contribute to their own security. The community does this by being actively present – noticing what is happening around them and reporting suspicious activity as necessary; however, home-sharing guests are inherently less attached to these communities and the need for communal security. After all, they are by nature away from home. As such, they are not going to have the same respect for the community as a homeowner (Gurran and Phibbs 2017).

Additionally, the residents of private homes or apartment buildings whose neighbors choose to share their home are not well suited to defend their spaces from high levels of strangers entering the community. For one, they are unlikely to be willing or prepared to do it. Many residents of these communities have purchased their properties with the expectation that there are stable homeowners among them, who don't often change.

Addressing the safety and security consequences of home sharing represents an unfair burden residents couldn't anticipate when buying their homes. As the Mayor of Ann Arbor stated: "People move into a residential neighborhood with the expectation that they will be surrounded by residents," as opposed to short-term visitors (Stanton 2020). This might not be problematic if hosts only share their homes sporadically, but in situations such as in Ann Arbor, where multiple properties are frequently shared to new people via home-sharing platforms, this can be a big disadvantage to the community's residents and also compromises their safety and security.

As a result, from a position of defensible space, home sharing not only presents multiple safety and security concerns to the community but also suggests some solutions. For example, if neighbors were alerted to the presence of a home share, they would be in a better position to keep watch on the property. Also, if the number of home shares in a neighborhood was capped, natural surveillance would not be as hindered as it might be in a neighborhood with unlimited numbers of home shares.

6.2 Rational Choice Theory Suggests Hotel and Home-Sharing Crime Can Be Prevented by Reducing Opportunities for Crime and Increasing Punishment for Bad Acts

Rational choice theory has been called one of the most powerful theories in social science (Ostrom 1975). It certainly can be praised for its simplicity and intuitive nature. This theory, based on economic principles, proposes that humans are motivated by their own personal benefit. When confronted with a choice of actions, they use a rational, calculated process, a cost-benefit analysis, to determine which choice provides them the greatest benefit and the least cost (Scott 2000; Elster 1986). In the context of criminology, rational choice theory would suggest that criminals are rational actors, seeking to benefit from their criminal behavior and making decisions whether or not to commit crime according to how much they will benefit versus the likelihood of getting caught and punished (Cornish and Clarke 1987).

Rational choice theory demonstrated that location is important to the criminal, and in the context of hotels and home sharing, it represents an opportunity that can be reduced. Rational choice theory reasons crime as a deliberate process. The locations where crime occurs are important to the offenders, because they serve as a "means to achieve their goals" (Eck and Weisburd 2015, p. 5; Cornish and Clarke 1989). The types of crimes that have been known to occur in home shares have been well deliberated. Specifically, two problematic crimes unique to home sharing, offering fake listings and illegally offering one's home for rent, demonstrate strong deliberation on the part of the criminal actor, as does using a home share to conduct criminal activity, which is another problem in the home-sharing space (see Chap. 3).

Based on rational choice theory, would-be criminals can be deterred. The fear of punishment, insofar as it is swift, certain, and severe in its application, is said to be effective in deterring criminals because the costs of punishment will outweigh the benefits derived from the crime (Kiltz and Ramsay 2012; Bailey and Smith 1972). Criminals, like most rational decision makers, will prefer to avoid significant pain and punishment. Based on this theory, policymakers often strive to deter crime by increasing the amount of penalty associated with the crime.

The other way to deter crime, according to this theory, is by increasing the likelihood that a criminal will get caught. In the security field, this is called target hardening. Target hardening measures, such as the presence of security guards, locks, alarms, barriers, and video surveillance, serve to decrease a target's chance of being selected for crime opportunities (Huang et al. 1998). These actions could serve to deter some of the illegal activities, such as operating illegal brothels or having drug parties, occurring in home share properties which the actors rented for this purpose.

It would seem in these instances, the actors specifically chose home shares instead of hotels, which are hardened targets, in that they have security presence, video surveillance, etc.

Rational Choice and Hotels The rational choice theory has been used in hotels to address many vulnerabilities. One example is electronic door locks, which record every entry into guest rooms. These locks deter would-be criminals because they will be more likely to be caught. In addition, most hotels have a single entry point for individuals who are not guests.

Another example is how hotels deal with the modern day security threat of terrorists. Hotels have frequently been the target of terroristic acts. One study documented 31 instances of international terroristic acts in hotels between 2002 and 2009 (Wernick and Glinow 2012). In one instance, on October 7, 2004, at a Hilton Hotel in Taba, Egypt, a suicide bomber drove a car filled with explosives into the lobby, killing 33 and injuring 150. Al-Qaeda was suspected to be the perpetrator in this crime. Another one happened on July 23, 2005, at Ghazala Gardens hotel in Sinai Peninsula, Egypt, where a truck bomb driven into the lobby killed 45 and injured 100. Abdullah Azzam Brigades was the suspected perpetrator (Wernick and Glinow 2012).

Criminologists argue that a terrorist is a rational criminal actor. They plan their crimes carefully, even low-level offenses choosing "specific crimes…for specific reasons" (Rossmo and Harries 2011; Cornish and Clarke 1987, p. 935). Wernick and Glinow (2012) argue that terrorists' interest in hotels as targets increased following the 9/11 attacks, because they symbolize "western affluence." They also are considered "soft targets" due to their accessibility to the public (p. 733–735).

Although terrorists may be rational actors, research has not concluded how best to deter them. Some scholars say punishment doesn't have the same deterrent effect on terrorists as it does on other types of criminals because of the nature of a terrorist's motivation (Kiltz and Ramsay 2012). One source of evidence is the phenomenon of suicidal terrorism (Caplan 2006). As a rational actor, a suicidal terrorist would conduct a cost-benefit analysis and determine their death was a cost, worthy of the benefit to the cause of damaging their enemy. In short, they hate their enemy more than they love themselves (Caplan 2006). Indeed, one study of jihadist suicide attackers showed they were driven by "the anticipation of future self-gratifying benefits" (Perry and Hasisi 2014; Freilich and LaFree 2014). Thus, when one's death is considered a benefit, it is hard to convince a person willing to die to think otherwise. That said, some scholars think that terrorists can be deterred, since millions of people believe they will be rewarded in the afterlife if they engage in a suicide attack; yet, few of these believers actually commit the crime (Caplan 2006).

Although terrorists are challenging to deter, hotels have employed many approaches to security to harden their facilities as a terroristic target. The goal is focusing on reducing opportunities while simultaneously increasing the resiliency of the physical environment, thereby improving the ability of the hotel to withstand and recover from an attack (Fussey 2009; Clarke and Newman 2006; Center for Internet Security 2020). Thus, hotels have implemented a number of provisions to reduce opportunity such as security surveillance cameras, physical presence of security guards, key card access to guest room floors in addition to guest rooms, and required training for all hotel staff to be universally proactive, serving as "partners of security officers in detection and enforcement" (Henderson et al. 2010).

Rational Choice and Home Sharing Under rational choice theory, home-sharing users who would commit crimes are assumed to be rational actors. As discussed in Chap. 3, these crimes range from bribery and extortion to fake listings and harassment to illegal brothels and drug use to subletting a sublet. These crimes demonstrate rational thought, as advance planning is required. As rational actors, these home-sharing users will weigh the costs and benefits before engaging in their crimes. This means, these criminals can also be deterred by increasing the costs of the crime in some way. But how? And who is responsible for deterring them?

Target hardening can deter certain crimes that might occur in a private residence. Both hosts and guests can play a role in this. Hosts can do as much as possible to ensure their property is not selected as a crime target. Visible security alarms, automatic lights, and strong locks can be useful. In addition, a host should only share space under their immediate control (think a homeowner sharing part or all of their own home, on occasion, as opposed to a landlord constantly sharing multiple properties in many locations). This type of host can alert the neighbors when they plan to have their home occupied by guests, so they can keep a watchful eye on the property and inform the host of any potential problems. A host can also harden the target of their home by offering key safety features such as a first aid kit and smoke alarms and noting their presence on their listing. This sends a message to potential criminals that their property is well maintained and monitored and, thus, is not an ideal target for criminal activity.

Guests can also take action to prevent themselves from being a target for unscrupulous hosts by carefully researching a listing to avoid booking a fake home share. As discussed in Chap. 3, a guest determined their listings were bogus after performing Google Image searches of the photos of the people and properties in the listing (Conti 2019). Another problematic issue, illegal listing, can also research the city and state where the listing is located to further verify what is required for a legal home share and ask the host questions about their listing.

However, some home-sharing-specific crimes can be difficult to deter. For example, hosts who post fake listings or illegally share their homes take a calculated risk to earn money, but the risk is relatively small because most guests will not do thorough research and will trust postings that look legitimate on the home-sharing company's platform. According to rational choice theory, for these crimes to be deterred, strong punishments would need to be enacted in order to dissuade bad acts.

Conclusions About Rational Choice Theory and Home Sharing Rational choice theory suggests that potential bad actors will choose the bad act if the benefits outway the costs based on the likelihood of getting caught and the punishment. Thus, a way to deter bad acts is to increase the likelihood that the bad actor will get caught and/or increase the punishment they will receive.

Using the lens of rational choice theory, we can see that both hosts and guests can take affirmative steps to harden the target at issue. These actions change the cost-benefit analysis of the potential bad actor who will think it more likely for them to be caught. Still, a change in the level of punishment for bad behavior in home sharing will require policy changes by the home-sharing company itself or local, state, and federal legislative bodies.

6.3 Routine Activity Theory Suggests That Guests of Both Hotels and Home Shares Can Thwart Crime

Routine activity theory was developed by Cohen and Felson in 1979. Their theory was unique at the time because they departed from the traditional approach to crime prevention by focusing solely on the offender (Kleemans et al. 2012). Cohen and Felson examined criminal events and activities, known today as situational crime prevention.

The three key elements of this theory are the offender, the target, and the guardian (1994). These elements make up what is known as the crime triangle (Kleemans et al. 2012). Under routine activity theory, crimes occur upon the convergence of (i) a motivated offender, (ii) a suitable target or victim, and (iii) in circumstances where the target lacks protection of a capable guardian. In other words, the paths of the victim and offender must intersect in time and space and in an environment that is conducive to criminal activity (Cohen and Felson 1979; Rossmo and Harries 2011). The theory posits that if any of these three components are missing, then crime will be unlikely to occur (Brunet 2002).

Under this theory, it is assumed there are always people available to do harm. Motivated offenders are considered ubiquitous (Groff 2007). As a result, crime prevention focuses on keeping motivated offenders away from targets by increasing the presence of capable guardians (Kleemans et al. 2012). Routine activity theorists ask probing questions such as "How do potential participants in crime routinely move through space and time in the course of the day?," which could provide insight into potential targets. Another question would be "Which hours of the day produce more of the routine activities that likely lead to crime?," which might help identify when guardians are more needed (Felson 1994, p. 147).

In the 1990s, Felson expanded on his original concept. Felson was studying criminal activity over time and space, looking for trends and patterns (1994), and he noticed that crime rates were influenced by people's lifestyles (Eck 2006; Felson 1994). The changing sociological landscape, such as the development of cities, the decreasing size of schools, the proliferation of people working from home, and the localization of social and economic environments, led to a change in criminal activity. He suggested that these types of changes increased guardianship, which decreased crime (Eck 2006).

Routine Activity Theory and Hotels Scholars have suggested that routine activity theory, along with defensible space theory, best explains hotel crimes (Huang et al. 1998). That's because guests, both potential criminal bad actors and potential victims, converge, creating an environment that is theoretically ripe for crime. Thus, this theory would suggest that to prevent crime from happening in a hotel, capable guardians must be present. In fact, formal guardians such as security guards, and other uniformed personnel, have been found to have the most influence, because they are most likely to intervene (Groff 2007). Therefore, hotels with a visible presence of security should make crime less likely to occur.

Hotels also have an inherent security advantage in preventing crime because they have multiple guardians present 24 h a day. Such guardians are trained professionals in matters of safety and security. Further, a hotel's guardians never leave when their property is inhabited by guests. Hotels also have many personnel who are considered "place managers" that "organize their place's physical environment and social processes to prevent crime" (Sampson et al. 2010; Eck 1995). In the hotel setting, these place managers could include janitors and bartenders along with other staff (Sampson et al. 2010; Eck 1995).

Hotels also often benefit from increased surveillance and patrol on the part of local law enforcement. Patrols help officers become familiar with hotels on their beat, giving them the ability to "recognize at a glance" whether "what is going on with them is within the range of normalcy" (Sherman et al. 1989, quoting Bittner 1989, p. 32).

Under routine activity theory, one could conclude that hotels are quite safe for honest guests because of the presence of multiple capable guardians. Yet, findings from a case study on hotel security by Brock and Walker (2008) also emphasize the role guests have regarding their own security (Brock and Walker 2008). Specifically, the researchers argue that guests' "safety/security is primarily in their own hands" (Brock and Walker 2008, p. 152). The reason why these researchers place the onus on guests to practice self-protection is because they suggest people "set themselves up as a suitable target, absent a capable guardian, in a sea of motivated offenders which they are either ignorant of, or refuse to consider important, relevant, or otherwise a threat." (Brock and Walker 2008, p. 144).

Under this application of routine activity theory, most housekeepers can be considered motivated offenders if they are paid low wages (Brock and Walker 2008). Targets are the guests who leave valuable belongings in their room. Even though hotel security and administrative staff serve as guardians for the hotel, they are not and cannot be present in hotel rooms. To provide a measure of target hardening, many hotels provide safes, either in the room or available at the front desk; however, the guest has the responsibility to actually secure their belongings. This research finds that hotel patrons are "not as careful" as they should be, when it comes to protecting their personal belongings. Brock and Walker's study concluded that guests need to practice more "self-security" when staying at hotels (2008, p. 144).

In summary, routine activity theory suggests that hotels are a subject to a high risk of crime due to the number of people passing through their doors and the number of employees who have access to private rooms. On the other hand, hotels have a lower risk than other locations due to the presence of security personnel and others, including various staff and local law enforcement, who can contribute to surveillance. Nevertheless, guests have a responsibility to contribute to their own safety and security when at a hotel.

Routine Activity Theory and Home Sharing Routine activity theory is focused on the geography of crime. Under routine activity theory, crime happens when a victim and offender converge in the same "activity space" (Xu et al. 2017, p. 2). In home sharing, the geography is very personal. The activity space is one's local community. The location of potential crimes, whether to hosts and their property or to guests and their property, is either someone's private residence or online. Crimes can take place in person or electronically. Potential victims may be victimized by the very people with whom they are transacting (host and guest) and involve a property owned or managed by one of the parties in the transaction. In hotels, in contrast, crime occurs at a commercial location that is not owned by any of the parties engaged in the transaction.

Using the lens of routine activity theory, home sharing presents multiple red flags when it comes to risk of crime. First, when a host opens up their home to many different people, they are exposing themselves to a wide range of potential criminal offenders. Routine activity theory explains how the "structural change" of a community, such as the presence of Airbnb listings, may induce criminal acts (Han and Wang 2019; Eck and Weisburd 2015). There are many cases where the guest themselves has exploited their status as a home-sharing guest to commit crimes of varying degrees on and against the property itself. These crimes have included hosting illegal brothels (Sauchelli and Golding 2014; Nyheter 2016; BBC 2017), filming pornographic videos (Susko and Schrader 2016; Associated Press 2018), hosting house parties (Yakowicz 2017) and sex parties (Rosario et al. 2014), housing drug labs (Karp 2020) and drug delivery services (Moyer and Hsu 2018), and facilitating human trafficking (Marchildon 2018).

Second, an issue arises with a lack of multiple, capable guardians. In the cases where a host is not present, there is an absence of a key guardian. Homeowners play an important role in protecting their homes (Sampson et al. 2010). In fact, research has found a correlation between homeowners spending time away from home and increased crime (Groff 2007). A home without the original homeowners present will be seen as a better crime target – to both the potential outside criminal actor and the guests themselves. Hosts who remain on the property while sharing their home could be considered place managers, who provide some security with their presence, but many do not.

In home sharing, whether the host is present or not, guests end up serving as a substitute guardian of sorts for the property, a role they may not be well-suited to assume, in particular because they do not have a vested interest in the property. Further, like hotel guests, home-sharing guests must take on a measure of self-protection. The ability to self-protect is an important characteristic that influences target suitability (Groff 2007); however, guests may feel relaxed and less responsible because of the homely setting maintained by another.

Other than hosts and guests, guardianship under this theory could also include neighborly behavior, when neighbors look out for each other and their respective properties (Sampson et al. 2010). This guardianship can occur "intentionally or unintentionally" (Sampson et al. 2010; Cohen and Felson 1979). However, this type of guardianship is hampered when neighbors are unable to readily recognize people who do not belong in the neighborhood due to home sharing.

The most visible form of guardianship is police or security guard presence, but private homes often do not have a law enforcement presence. Sometimes, security patrols occur in private communities, whether provided by private security companies or through a contract with the police, but it is likely more rare that these properties would permit or partake in home sharing. In short, home sharing occurs in places where there is a distinct lack of multiple, capable guardians.

Third, neither hosts nor guests should be assumed to be experts in security who can take steps toward target hardening. Situational crime prevention requires increasing effort, increasing risk, reducing rewards, reducing provocation, and removing excuses (Felson and Clarke 1998). Examples of successful situational crime prevention measures include surveillance cameras in parking facilities, defensible space architecture in public housing, and target hardening of apartment blocks (Clarke 1995). For similar strategies to be implemented in a private home could be challenging and costly to hosts and guests.

Conclusions About Routine Activity Theory and Home Sharing This theory suggests guests of hotels and home sharing are ultimately responsible for protecting themselves against crime. External guardianship should not be presumed, because "much guardianship is self-guardianship – people taking action to protect themselves" (Sampson et al. 2010). Policymakers can use this information to help reduce the potential number of crime victims in home sharing through public outreach aimed at educating hosts and guests how to increase the situational awareness and improve their roles as guardians.

6.4 Conclusion

This chapter discusses several criminological theories as they apply to the subject of security in hotels and home shares. As this information shows, security is a complex discipline. While no theory can completely explain why crime occurs, many theories can come together to provide insight into crime and criminals. The theories discussed here provide many important takeaways for hotel guests and users of home-sharing services. They help explain why home sharing by its very nature makes users more vulnerable to crime and provides guidance to home-sharing users (and hotel guests) how to reduce their level of risk.

The theories also provide some important considerations for policymakers. For example, these theories suggest that capping the number of home shares in a neighborhood can help prevent the loss of a sense of neighborhood identity, which fosters neighbors performing informal surveillance of the area. Also, defining home-sharing-related crimes and establishing levels of punishment for them should deter many bad actors. Finally, public awareness campaigns could serve to educate home-sharing users both hosts and guests how to proactively protect themselves and their property from harm.

The next chapter furthers our understanding of safety in home sharing with a review of the impact of COVID-19 on the hospitality industry. As might be expected, this pandemic exposed issues not previously considered. This review is used to develop further guidance for users and policymakers, which can be found in Chap. 8.

Works Cited

Associated Press. (2018). Woman sues after rental home was used to shoot pornography. *AP News.com*. Retrieved from https://apnews.com/577f18febd334b18b5c8fa0feacd370c

Atlas, R. (1991, March). The other side of CPTED. *Security Management Magazine*. Retrieved from https://www.cpted-security.com/wp-content/uploads/the_other_side_cpted.pdf on March 1, 2020.

Bailey, W. C., & Smith, R. W. (1972). Punishment: Its severity and certainty. *Journal of Criminal Law, Criminology, and Police Science, 63*, 530.

Barber, M. (2016, November 10). Airbnb vs. the city. *Curbed*. Retrieved from https://www.curbed.com/2016/11/10/13582982/airbnb-laws-us-cities on July 0, 2020.

BBC. (2017). My Airbnb flat was turned into a popup brothel. *BBC.com*. Retrieved from https://www.bbc.com/news/magazine-39528479

Brock, D., & Walker, D. (2008). Hotel security and the routine activities approach. *The Police Journal: Theory, Practice and Principles, 81*(2), 144–153. https://doi.org/10.1350/pojo.2008.81.2.391.

Brunet, J. R. (2002). Discouragement of crime through civil remedies: An application of a reformulated routine activities theory. *Western Criminology Review, 4*, 68.

Burgen, S. (2020). Soaring rents and noisy parties: How Airbnb is forcing out Barcelona locals. *The Guardian*. Retrieved from https://www.theguardian.com/technology/2020/feb/20/soaring-rents-and-noisy-parties-how-airbnb-is-forcing-out-barcelona-locals

Caplan, B. (2006). Terrorism: The relevance of the rational choice model. *Public Choice, 128*(1–2), 91–107.

Center for Internet Security. (2020). A short guide to infrastructure security and resiliency. *CIS Security*. Retrieved from https://www.cisecurity.org/blog/a-short-guide-to-infrastructure-security-and-resiliency/#:~:text=The%20term%20'resilience'%20means%20the,naturally%20occurring%20threats%20or%20incidents on July 9, 2020.

Chavarria, L. (2019, November 4). Chicagoans push for more rules in response to Airbnb 'party house' ban. *NBCChicago.com*. Retrieved from https://www.nbcchicago.com/news/local/chicago-ban-airbnb-house-party/2079227/ on July 9, 2020.

Clarke, R. V. (1995). Situational crime prevention. *Crime and Justice, 19*, 91–150. https://doi.org/10.1086/449230.

Clarke, R. V. G., & Newman, G. R. (2006). *Outsmarting the terrorists* (Vol. 144). Westport: Praeger Security International.

Cohen, L. E., & Felson, M. (1979). Social change and crime rate trends: A routine activity approach. *American Sociological Review, 44*(4), 588–608. https://doi.org/10.2307/2094589.
Conti, A. (2019). I accidentally uncovered a nationwide scam on Airbnb. *Vice.com*. Retrieved from https://www.vice.com/en_us/article/43k7z3/nationwide-fake-host-scam-on-airbnb
Cornish, D. B., & Clarke, R. V. (1987). Understanding crime displacement: An application of rational choice theory. *Criminology, 25*(4), 933–948. https://doi.org/10.1111/j.1745-9125.1987.tb00826.x.
Cornish, D. B., & Clarke, R. V. (1989). Crime specialisation, crime displacement and rational choice theory. In *Criminal behavior and the justice system research in criminology* (pp. 103–117). New York: Springer. https://doi.org/10.1007/978-3-642-86017-1_7.
Cowley, J., Agro, C., & McDonald, J. (2019, March 23). 'I felt like a criminal': Airbnb hosts ask guests to lie, sneak around in covert rentals. *CBC News*. Retrieved from https://www.cbc.ca/news/business/marketplace-airbnb-covert-listings-banned-units-1.5066673 on July 9, 2020.
Docklands News. (2020). "We live here" March 2020. *Docklands News*. Retrieved from: https://www.docklandsnews.com.au/columns/detail/we-live-here-march-2020_16142/
Dong, H. (2017). Does walkability undermine neighbourhood safety? *Journal of Urban Design, 22*(1), 59–75.
Duffala, D. C. (1976). Convenience stores, armed robbery, and physical environmental features. *American Behavioral Scientist, 20*(2), 227–245.
Durbin, D. A. (2019). Airbnb says it's banning 'party houses' after a shooting at a Halloween party in California killed 5 people. *Business Insider*. Retrieved from https://www.businessinsider.com/airbnb-ceo-says-company-is-banning-party-houses-2019-11
Eck, J. E. (1995). Examining routine activity theory: A review of two books. *Justice Quarterly, 12*(4), 783–797. https://doi.org/10.1080/07418829500096301.
Eck, J. E. (2006). When is a bologna sandwich better than sex? A defense of small-n case study evaluations. *Journal of Experimental Criminology, 2*(3), 345–362.
Eck, J. E., & Weisburd, D. (2015). Crime places in crime theory. *Crime and Place: Crime Prevention Studies, 4*, 1–33.
Ellery, B., Powell, M., & Atkinson, A. (2018, December 30). How Airbnb bandits rent out properties to prostitutes, drug dealers and party animals. *Dailymail.com*. Retrieved from https://www.dailymail.co.uk/news/article-6538881/How-Airbnb-bandits-rent-properties-prostitutes-drug-dealers-party-animals.html on July 4, 2020.
Elster, J. (1986). *Rational choice*. New York: New York University Press.
Felson, M. (1994). *Crime and everyday life: Insights and implications for society*. Thousand Oaks: Sage.
Felson, M., & Clarke, R. V. (1998). *Opportunity makes the thief: Practical theory for crime prevention* (Police Research Series, 98). Policing and Reducing Crime Unit, Research, Development and Statistics Directorate.
Freilich, J. D., & Lafree, G. (2014). Criminology theory and terrorism: Introduction to the special issue. *Terrorism and Political Violence, 27*(1), 1–8. https://doi.org/10.1080/09546553.2014.959405.
Fussey, P. (2009). An economy of choice? Terrorist decision-making and criminological rational choice theories reconsidered. *Security Journal, 24*(1), 85–99. https://doi.org/10.1057/sj.2009.11.
Greenberg, S. W., Rohe, W. M., & Williams, J. R. (1982). *Safe and secure neighborhoods: Physical characteristics and informal territorial control in high and low crime neighborhoods*. Washington, DC: Department of Justice, National Institute of Justice.
Groff, E. R. (2007). Simulation for theory testing and experimentation: An example using routine activity theory and street robbery. *Journal of Quantitative Criminology, 23*(2), 75–103. https://doi.org/10.1007/s10940-006-9021-z.
Gurran, N., & Phibbs, P. (2017). When tourists move in: How should urban planners respond to Airbnb? *Journal of the American Planning Association, 83*(1), 80–92.
Han, W., & Wang, X. (2019). Does home sharing impact crime rate? A tale of two cities. *Proceedings of the international conference on information systems*, Munich, Germany. Retrieved from https://aisel.aisnet.org/icis2019/sustainable_is/sustainable_is/6/ on July 3, 2020.

Henderson, J. C., Shufen, C., Huifen, L., & Xiang, L. L. (2010). Tourism and terrorism: A hotel industry perspective. *Journal of Tourism, Hospitality and Culinary Arts (JTHCA), 2*(1), 1–14.

Huang, W. S. W., Kwag, M., & Streib, G. (1998). Exploring the relationship between hotel characteristics and crime. *Hospitality Review, 16*(1), Article 9. Retrieved from https://digitalcommons.fiu.edu/hospitalityreview/vol16/iss1/9 on July 3, 2020.

Karp, C. (2020). Man, 28, rents an apartment on Airbnb and uses it to house an intricate Breaking Bad-style meth lab. *Daily Mail.* Retrieved from https://www.dailymail.co.uk/news/article-8589723/Man-rents-Airbnb-unit-create-intricate-Breaking-Bad-style-meth-lab.html

Kiltz, L., & Ramsay, J. D. (2012). Perceptual framing of homeland security. *Homeland Security Affairs, 8*(16), 1–27. Retrieved from https://www.hsaj.org/articles/230 on July 10, 2020.

Kleemans, E. R., Soudijn, M., & Weenink, A. (2012). Organized crime, situational crime prevention and routine activity theory. *Trends in Organized Crime, 15*(2–3), 87–92. https://doi.org/10.1007/s12117-012-9173-1.

Marchildon, J. (2018, February 23). Airbnb rentals are increasingly being used for human trafficking, police say. *Global Citizen.* Retrieved from www.globalcitizen.org/en/content/airbnb-human-trafficking/ on July 3, 2020.

Merry, S. E. (1981). Defensible space undefended. *Urban Affairs Quarterly, 16*(4), 397–422. https://doi.org/10.1177/107808748101600401.

Molumby, T. (1976). Patterns of crime in a university housing project. *American Behavioral Scientist, 20*(2), 247–259.

Moyer, J., & Hsu, S. (2018). Man used Airbnb sites to stash marijuana in door-to-door delivery operation, authorities say. *The Washington Post.* Retrieved from https://webcache.googleusercontent.com/search?q=cache:svdGWLDIlG4J:https://www.washingtonpost.com/local/public-safety/man-used-airbnb-sites-to-stash-marijuana-in-door-to-door-delivery-operation-authorities-contend/2018/11/02/5e0166ba-deb6-11e8-8c8c-0ba13dcb935a_story.html+&cd=1&hl=en&ct=clnk&gl=us

Newman, O. (1972). *Defensible space* (p. 264). New York: Macmillan.

Nyheter, D. (2016). Stockholm prostitutes use Airbnb to set up makeshift brothels. *Worldcrunch.com.* Retrieved from https://worldcrunch.com/blog/stockholm-prostitutes-use-airbnb-to-set-up-makeshift-brothels

Ostrom, V. (1975). Defensible space: Crime prevention through urban design, by Ocar Newman. *American Political Science Review, 69*(1), 279–280. https://doi.org/10.2307/1957945.

Perry, S., & Hasisi, B. (2014). Rational choice rewards and the jihadist suicide bomber. *Terrorism and Political Violence, 27*(1), 53–80. https://doi.org/10.1080/09546553.2014.962991.

Plautz, J. (2015, May 1). NYC politician goes undercover at Airbnb listings in illegal hotel sting. *Mashable.* Retrieved from https://mashable.com/2015/05/01/airbnb-sting-new-york-city/ on July 4, 2020.

Pyle, G. F. (1976). Spatial and temporal aspects of crime in Cleveland, Ohio. *American Behavioral Scientist, 20*(2), 175–198.

Repetto, T. A. (1976). Crime prevention through environmental policy: A critique. *American Behavioral Scientist, 20*, 275–288.

Reynald, D. M., & Elffers, H. (2009). The future of Newman's defensible space theory. *European Journal of Criminology, 6*(1), 25–46. https://doi.org/10.1177/1477370808098103.

Rosario, F., Sullivan, C. J., & Tacopino, J. (2014). Airbnb renter returns to 'overweight orgy.' *NY Post.* Retrieved from https://nypost.com/2014/03/17/airbnb-renter-claims-he-returned-home-to-an-orgy/

Rosenbaum, D. P. (1987). The theory and research behind neighborhood watch: Is it a sound fear and crime reduction strategy? *Crime & Delinquency, 33*(1), 103–134. https://doi.org/10.1177/0011128787033001007.

Rossmo, D. K., & Harries, K. (2011). The geospatial structure of terrorist cells. *Justice Quarterly, 28*(2), 221–248. https://doi.org/10.1080/07418820903426197.

Sampson, R., Eck, J. E., & Dunham, J. (2010). Super controllers and crime prevention: A routine activity explanation of crime prevention success and failure. *Security Journal, 23*(1), 37–51.

Sauchelli, D., & Golding, B. (2014, April 14). Hookers turning Airbnb apartments into brothels. *New York Post.* Retrieved from https://nypost.com/2014/04/14/hookers-using-airbnb-to-use-apartments-for-sex-sessions/ on July 4, 2020.

Scott, J. (2000). Rational choice theory. In *Understanding contemporary society: Theories of the present* (pp. 126–138). London: Sage. https://doi.org/10.4135/9781446218310.n9.

Sherman, L. W., Patrick, G. R., & Buerger, M. E. (1989). Hot spots of predatory crime: Routine activities and the criminology of place. *Criminology, 27*(1), 27–56. https://doi.org/10.1111/j.1745-9125.1989.tb00862.x.

Skogan, W. G. (1981). *Issues in the measurement of victimization* (Vol. 74682). Washington, DC: US Department of Justice, Bureau of Justice Statistics.

Spielman, F. (2020). Top mayoral aide vows massive re-write of Chicago's home sharing ordinance. *Chicago Sun Times.* Retrieved from https://chicago.suntimes.com/city-hall/2020/3/4/21165254/airbnb-rentals-neighbors-complaints-home-sharing-ordinance

Stafford, M., Chandola, T., & Marmot, M. (2007). Association between fear of crime and mental health and physical functioning. *American Journal of Public Health, 97*(11), 2076–2081.

Stanton, R. (2019a, October 3). Ann Arbor exploring regulations for Airbnb short-term rentals. *MLive.* Retrieved from https://www.mlive.com/news/ann-arbor/2019/10/ann-arbor-exploring-regulations-for-airbnb-short-term-rentals.html on July 10, 2020.

Stanton, R. (2019b, October 7). Ann Arbor residents divided on adding regulations for Airbnb short term rentals. *MLive.* Retrieved from https://www.mlive.com/news/ann-arbor/2019/10/ann-arbor-residents-divided-on-adding-regulations-for-airbnb-short-term-rentals.html on July 10, 2020.

Stanton, R. (2020, January 8). Ann Arbor may ban dedicated Airbnb short-term rental properties. *MLive.* Retrieved from https://www.mlive.com/news/ann-arbor/2020/01/ann-arbor-may-ban-dedicated-airbnb-short-term-rental-properties.html on July 10, 2020.

Susko, J., & Schrader, M. (2016). Porn industry sues Airbnb, rental houses for filming. *NBC Los Angeles.* Retrieved from https://www.nbclosangeles.com/news/local/porn-industry-uses-airbnb-rental-houses-for-filming/2086679/

Toler, C. (2020). New city task force may not solve Airbnb nuisance, neighbors say. *Advocate Lake Highlands.* Retrieved from https://lakehighlands.advocatemag.com/2020/02/new-city-task-force-may-not-solve-airbnb-nuisance-neighbors-say/

Wernick, D. A., & Von Glinow, M. A. (2012). Reflections on the evolving terrorist threat to luxury hotels: A case study on Marriott International. *Thunderbird International Business Review, 54*(5), 729–746.

Wiśniewska, A. (2019). Are Airbnb investors destroying Europe's cultural capitals? *Financial Times.* Retrieved from https://www.ft.com/content/2fe06a7c-cb2a-11e9-af46-b09e8bfe60c0

Xu, Y. H., Kim, J. W., & Pennington-Gray, L. (2017). Explore the spatial relationship between Airbnb rental and crime. *Proceedings from travel and tourism research association: Advancing tourism research globally.* Retrieved from https://scholarworks.umass.edu/cgi/viewcontent.cgi?article=2075andcontext=ttra on July 3, 2020.

Yakowicz, W. Inc. (2017, December 7). How an entrepreneur turned an Airbnb 'sex party' into a viral hit. *HuffPost.* Retrieved from www.huffpost.com/entry/airbnb-freak-fest_n_5063969 on July 10, 2020.

Chapter 7
What Issues About Home Sharing Has the Advent of COVID-19 Exposed?

The coronavirus (also known as COVID-19 or SARs-CoV-2) is a rare but easily spreading virus initially detected in Wuhan, China, and reported publicly on December 31, 2019. The disease quickly became a worldwide pandemic, with its presence reported in the United States by the Centers for Disease Control and Prevention (CDC) on January 20, 2020. The COVID-19 outbreak was declared a public health emergency of international concern by the World Health Organization (WHO) on January 30, 2020. At the time of this writing, there have been 7.9 million confirmed cases and over 430,000 deaths across the world (WHO, June 15, 2020). The United States has experienced over 2.3 million cases and over 121,000 deaths (CDC 2020). Although a lot is not yet known about the virus, such as how it is transmitted and how it attacks the body, due to the high volume of cases, it is suspected that it transmits very easily, perhaps by remaining on surfaces and through close contact with an infected person. As a result, much of the public around the world was advised to stay home, with limited exceptions, remain 6 feet apart from others, and wear a face covering/mask.

The advent of COVID-19 effectively suspended the entire travel industry. It made it very difficult, if not illegal, to travel. There were "lockdown" orders by many government bodies, which precluded people from traveling. In New York, which was initially considered the "epicenter" of the pandemic in the United States, citizens were told that they should *all* assume they were exposed to the virus (Brown and Marsh 2020; McKinley 2020). Other states insisted that anyone traveling from New York to quarantine themselves for a 2-week period at their expense (Hawai'i Tourism Authority 2020; Oliveria 2020). These types of requirements made the prospect of traveling very expensive, not to mention personally onerous. As a result, people largely refrained from traveling and stayed at home while waiting for the worst part of the epidemic to pass.

Hotels were also deeply affected by the pandemic. In many jurisdictions, hotels were deemed nonessential and, therefore, ordered closed (Ricca 2020). The hotel

C. A. Binns, R. J. Kempf, *Safety and Security in Hotels and Home Sharing*, SpringerBriefs in Criminology, https://doi.org/10.1007/978-3-030-59306-3_7

industry reportedly lost $2 billion in weekly wages, with 8 out of 10 hotel rooms empty in April 2020 (Carter 2020). Cleaning and sanitizing became a top priority. Marriott adopted surgical grade disinfectants, Hilton partnered with Lysol and the Mayo Clinic to plan its cleaning standards, and Hyatt created an accreditation program for its employees focusing on cleaning and disinfecting (Compton 2020). As a travel risk management consultant started early on in the pandemic: "Hotels need to instill confidence in their guests and staff that they are acting responsibly" (Fox 2020).

Even with new cleaning standards, evidence suggests that major hotels such as Marriott and Hilton were refunding most bookings, even those reservations that were "nonrefundable." Also many major hotel chains reportedly allowed guests to rebook for free, waived cancellation fees and allowed guests to delay payment – all up until 24 h before their stay (Walker 2020). These actions should serve to placate panicked guests and encourage brand loyalty (Mastrogiacomo 2020).

The pandemic also hit home sharing hard. Airbnb's loss was staggering. The company reportedly lost $1.5 billion in bookings in mid-March due to the pandemic (Halpern 2020; Mickle and Rana 2020). Since then, Airbnb has laid off 1900 people, representing 25% of their workforce (Halpern 2020). Many guests were unable to travel, and hosts were leery about sharing their home during a pandemic. The concern extended to the greater community as neighbors also worried about the risks of COVID-19 increasing with travelers entering their neighborhood or apartment building (Halpern 2020). Airbnb was banned in several cities and states to thwart the carrying of the virus across state lines (Rodriguez 2020).

COVID-19 brought attention to several safety risks, including the transmission and spread of the virus, that are elemental to home sharing. Hosts can be placed at risk if the guests are carrying the virus. Guests are at risk from catching the virus from either the host or a previous guest. The safety risk is even greater due to the fact that each host and each guest operates independently. Thus, cleanliness and other safety standards cannot be uniformly established nor can compliance be assured.

Airbnb has published guidance for hosts including a 14-step cleaning and disinfecting process and a list of items, such as light switches and door knobs, that need special attention when disinfecting (Airbnb 2020a). Airbnb also recommends providing certain amenities for guests, such as paper towels, soap, and hand sanitizer, which can help both parties reduce the risk of inflection. Finally, Airbnb suggests hosts allow at least 24 h between guests and consider providing a method of entry that requires no or low contact between guest and host. The company tells hosts: "Guests will want to know about all of the additional steps you're taking to reduce the spread of infection. So it's a good idea to mention your enhanced cleaning routine in your listing description" (Airbnb 2020a).

In terms of refunds and rescheduling, Airbnb's response was a bit more complicated. To understand what occurred, it is first important to understand how payment and refunds on Airbnb worked before the pandemic. In most instances, Airbnb guests pay for their stay up front after the host accepts the reservation request. The host then receives the money 24 h after the guest checks in. Airbnb holds the money in the interim, collecting a 14.2% service fee from the guest and approximately 3% service fee from the host[1] (Airbnb 2020c). The host chooses between four types of cancellation policies ranging from flexible (allowing for full refunds) to very strict (allowing for 50% refund), but only if the cancellation is made 60 days before the scheduled check-in date, but Airbnb generally keeps service fees.

In response to COVID-19, Airbnb instituted a new "extenuating circumstance" policy on March 19, 2020 (Airbnb 2020b). That policy allowed any reservations for stays made on or before March 14, 2020, with a check-in date between March 14, 2020, and July 31, 2020, could be canceled by either the guest or host before check-in. Guests who cancelled would receive a full cash refund, including service fees, or a travel credit in the same amount. Hosts who cancelled would not threaten their Superhost status, which is in part based on low numbers of cancellations.

Airbnb's policy went on to address cancellations after March 14, 2020. The policy noted that after that date, the presence of COVID-19 was no longer to be considered an extenuating circumstance because the impact of the pandemic on travel could be foreseen. Specifically, the following COVID-19-related circumstances are not considered extenuating under the policy: "transportation disruptions and cancellations; travel advisories and restrictions; health advisories and quarantines; changes to applicable law; and other government mandates—like evacuation orders, border closures, prohibitions on short-term rentals, and shelter-in-place requirements" (Airbnb 2020b). The only exception is if the host or guest contracts the virus. Otherwise, the host's cancellation policy would apply.

While some guests are undoubtedly happy to receive full refunds according to the policy, these guests have been less vocal. The guests who have reached out to the media to complain had reservations that were scheduled outside of Airbnb's refund window. These guests are very unhappy particularly about hosts whose cancellation policies only allowed them a 50% refund even if they were confronted by travel bans or quarantine orders, which made nonessential travel impossible.

One example is a guest from Surrey, UK, who had planned to attend a May, 2020, wedding in Hawaii and booked his trip in October, 2019. He found he was not eligible for a full refund under Airbnb's extenuating circumstance policy, because he cancelled after March 14. He attributed his cancellation to multiple reasons: the wedding was cancelled because the Hawaiian government decided to prohibit gatherings of more than 10 people to prevent the spread of COVID-19 (Hawai'i Tourism Authority 2020); the state also required anyone entering the state to self-quarantine for a 2-week period; and the guest's home country instituted a travel ban (Steacy and MacMahon 2020). After all that, he only could receive a refund if the host agreed to provide him one, which in this case, they didn't. Instead, his host decided to adhere to their cancellation policy, which would only provide him with a 50% refund.

Hosts have also complained about Airbnb's extenuating circumstance policy. The Airbnb Twitter Help page was flooded with complaints from users who were

[1] The host's fee is higher in some instances.

unable to collect their desired refund. The general issue has to do with Airbnb allowing full refunds for cancellations made on March 14 or later, which caused some hosts a significant loss of income. They have argued that they had no notice of the change of policy and think Airbnb should not have been able to override their individual refund policies, because they lost a significant income. Hosts who purchased homes for the sole purpose of renting them out on home-sharing platforms have suffered the greatest losses. Without their rental income, these hosts are unable to pay their mortgages.

7.1 Conclusion

The advent of COVID-19 has exposed problems with the decentralized structure of home sharing. The independence of hosts leads to difficulties with ensuring that home shares are cleaned and disinfected effectively and consistently. Likewise, given the autonomy of hosts and guests, it is not surprising that Airbnb's imposition of new policies received pushback. Potential solutions to these problems, along with others discussed in previous chapters, will be discussed in the concluding chapter.

Works Cited

Airbnb. (2020a). Cleaning guidelines to help prevent the spread of COVID-19. *Airbnb.com*. Retrieved from https://www.airbnb.com/resources/hosting-homes/a/cleaning-guidelines-to-help-prevent-the-spread-of-covid-19-163 on June 26, 2020.

Airbnb. (2020b). Extenuating circumstances policy and the coronavirus (COVID-19). *Airbnb.com*. Retrieved from https://www.airbnb.com/help/article/2701/extenuating-circumstances-policy-and-the-coronavirus-covid19 on June 26, 2020.

Airbnb. (2020c) What is the Airbnb service fee? *Airbnb.com*. Retrieved from https://www.airbnb.com/help/article/1857/what-is-the-airbnb-service-fee#:~:text=Guest%20service%20fee,before%20they%20book%20a%20reservation on June 28, 2020.

Brown, L., & Marsh, J. (2020). New Yorkers should assume they've been exposed to coronavirus: Officials. *New York Post*, March 16. Retrieved from https://nypost.com/2020/03/15/new-yorkers-should-assume-theyve-been-exposed-to-coronavirus-officials/ on July 10, 2020.

Carter, S. M. (2020). Hotels hit hard in coronavirus pandemic, lose $2B in weekly wages. *Fox Business*, April 24. Retrieved from https://www.foxbusiness.com/lifestyle/hotels-hit-hard-in-coronavirus-pandemic-losing-2b-in-weekly-wages on July 10, 2020.

Centers for Disease Control and Prevention. (2020). United States COVID-19 cases and deaths by state on CDC COVID Data Tracker. *Centers for Disease Control and Prevention*. Retrieved from https://www.cdc.gov/covid-data-tracker/#cases on June 25, 2020.

Compton, N. B. (2020). What hotels are doing to sanitize rooms during the pandemic. *The Statesman*, May 8. Retrieved from https://www.statesman.com/entertainmentlife/20200508/what-hotels-are-doing-to-sanitize-rooms-during-pandemic on July 7, 2020.

Fox, J. T. (2020). How hotel companies are working to lessen coronavirus impact. *Hotel Management*. Retrieved from https://www.hotelmanagement.net/operate/hotels-respond-to-coronavirus-threat on June 26, 2020.

Halpern, A. (2020). How Airbnb could change after the pandemic-for the better. *Conde Nast Travel*, May 19. Retrieved from https://www.cntraveler.com/story/how-airbnb-could-change-after-the-pandemic-for-the-better on July 10, 2020.

Hawai'i Tourism Authority. (2020). COVID-19 mandatory 14 day quarantine for all arriving passengers. Hawai'i Tourism Authority. Retrieved from https://www.hawaiitourismauthority.org/news/alerts/covid-19-novel-coronavirus/ on June 17, 2020.

Mastrogiacomo, M. (2020). COVID-19 hotel recovery strategy: Top 10 digital strategies while travel is on pause. *Next Guest*, April 13. Retrieved from https://www.nextguest.com/blog/covid-19-hotel-recovery-strategy-top-10-digital-strategies-while-travel-is-on-pause/ on July 10, 2020.

McKinley, J. (2020). New York City region is now an epicenter of the coronavirus pandemic. *The New York Times*. Retrieved from https://www.nytimes.com/2020/03/22/nyregion/Coronavirus-new-York-epicenter.html

Mickle, T., & Rana, P. (2020, April 28). 'A Bargain with the devil'-bill comes due for overextended Airbnb hosts. *Wall Street Journal*, April 28. Retrieved from https://www.wsj.com/articles/a-bargain-with-the-devilbill-comes-due-for-overextended-airbnb-hosts-11588083336 on July 10, 2020.

Oliveria, N. (2020). Florida orders all visitors from NYC area to self-quarantine for 2 weeks. *The Daily News*. Retrieved from https://www.nydailynews.com/coronavirus/ny-coronavirus-florida-orders-nyc-area-visitors-to-self-quarantine-20200324-6knewexndbap7hqjruyoyflsgu-story.html

Ricca, S. (2020). Following COVID-19 developments, industry's response. *Hotel News Now,* June 17. Retrieved from https://www.hotelnewsnow.com/Articles/300779/Following-COVID-19-developments-industrys-response on July 10, 2020.

Rodriguez, S. (2020). Airbnb hosts feel the crunch of coronavirus as governments ban short-term rentals. *CNBC*. Retrieved from https://www.cnbc.com/2020/04/16/airbnb-hosts-feel-the-crunch-of-coronavirus-short-term-rental-bans.html

Steacy, L., & MacMahon, M. (2020). 'This is unfair': Surrey man frustrated with Airbnb refusal to refund Hawaii booking. *City News,* March 29. Retrieved from https://www.citynews1130.com/2020/03/28/hawaii-airbnb-refund-covid-19/ on July 10, 2020.

Walker, V. M. (2020). What you need to know about coronavirus hotel change and cancellation policies. *The Points Guy*, June 3. Retrieved from https://thepointsguy.com/guide/coronavirus-hotel-change-cancellation-policies/ on July 10, 2020.

World Health Organization, Coronavirus disease. Retrieved from https://www.who.int/emergencies/diseases/novel-coronavirus-2019 on June 15, 2020.

Chapter 8
Conclusions, Policy Recommendations, Limitations, and Suggestions for Future Research

This brief has examined issues of safety and security in home shares, using the approach to safety and security in hotels as a baseline for comparison. Home sharing has disrupted the hospitality industry to a great degree given its relatively recent entry into the market. Home-sharing companies connect hosts who wish to share some portion or all of their home to guests visiting an area. Generally, the cost is lower than hotels for guests, and they get to experience a unique, homely experience. Home sharing, part of the new gig economy arising from Internet platforms connecting sellers with buyers, has provided hosts with a new source of income around the world.

Yet, evidence shows that home sharing is similarly vulnerable to crimes and accidents as hotels. Even though there is a lack of current quantitative data for safety and security incidents in either location, anecdotal reports show that home-sharing guests can be subject to a range of security problems from discrimination and harassment to assault and murder. In addition, home-sharing hosts have experienced problems with misbehaving guests as well. Guests have destroyed property, harassed hosts, and squatted in place. All of these crimes could conceivably occur in a hotel setting; however, several new crimes unique to the home-sharing setting have emerged. They include hosts posting fake listings, hosts posting listings when they are not legal in the locality, and guests exploiting the privacy of a private home to perform illegal acts on hosts' property. Home shares are also vulnerable to safety concerns such as fire and earthquake.

Although hotels and home-sharing companies are generally concerned with preventing similar crimes and accidents, the legal context for each varies considerably. In the United States, hotels are subject to a long-standing set of expectations based on Innkeeper Laws originally developed in England. These laws, primarily developed in case law, place a large share of responsibility on hotels to take steps to keep their guests and the guests' property safe and secure. Hotels are also subject to a plethora of rules and regulations that they must comply with, from accommodation of individuals with disabilities to fire safety.

C. A. Binns, R. J. Kempf, *Safety and Security in Hotels and Home Sharing*, SpringerBriefs in Criminology, https://doi.org/10.1007/978-3-030-59306-3_8

Home-sharing companies are, in contrast, unregulated. As a legal matter, home-sharing companies currently enjoy a shield from liability under a federal law that was created to protect Internet platforms from being held responsible for the actions users take on their platform. As a result, even though home-sharing transactions are managed by home-sharing companies, the weight of the legal responsibility for preventing crimes and accidents and dealing with the aftermath of any bad events falls onto home-sharing hosts and guests.

Some states and cities in which home sharing has expanded rapidly have moved to try to regulate home sharing for multiple reasons, including loss of hotel tax revenue, the reduction of housing stock to time shares, and increased issues of safety and security. New York State and New York City, for example, have taken several steps to try to regulate home sharing, despite the federal law, by using health and safety laws to impose mandates on home shares, by fining landlords who allow home sharing to occur on their property, and by working with Airbnb in particular to get lists of home shares in the jurisdiction in order to verify they are legal. These approaches have had moderate success, but nevertheless, state and local policymakers have limited options, and hosts and guests lacking other remedies can only obtain legal protection through purchasing insurance or turning to courts of law.

With the backdrop of these disparate legal contexts, a number of safety and security practices have been developed by the hospitality field. Hotels' practices have evolved from focusing on crime happening on the premises to addressing loss prevention and ensuring guests, employees, and the property are safe and secure. So, in addition to complying with fire and other mandatory regulations, hotels implement a number of practices to improve the security and safety of guest rooms, the hotel itself, and the surrounding premises. Hotels also carefully vet employees, verify the identities of the guests, and pursue informal approaches to security, such as getting to know local law enforcement.

In contrast to hotels, home-sharing companies make recommendations to both hosts and guests about safety and security practices, but because of the decentralized nature of home sharing, there is no mechanism to ensure that appropriate practices have been put into place in home shares. Nevertheless, Airbnb, as an example, has worked to implement a secure website for communication and payment and has established a two-way rating system for guests and hosts to describe their experiences for other users. Airbnb also performs a brief background check of its users and shapes the terms of the guest-host relationship. Nevertheless, guests and hosts need to adopt their own practices. This brief provides a number of tips that individuals who participate in home sharing rather than staying in hotels can adopt to protect their safety and security in that setting.

The review of criminal activities, laws and regulations, and safety and security practices in the hospitality field demonstrates that the responsibility that is largely placed on a hotel to keep individuals and property safe and secure *shifts* to home-sharing hosts and guests. Meanwhile, the home-sharing company that sets up the transaction has no responsibility or rather, no legal liability, to do so at all. The implications of this shift are examined through the lenses of several criminological theories to understand the weaknesses of the home-sharing system and how things could be addressed to reduce the risk of crime and accidents. All these theories not only identify problems inherent in the home-sharing setting but also suggest policy actions.

Defensible space theory posits that a locality can be specifically designed to reduce crime. Most hotels have adopted multiple defensible space techniques that naturally encourage increased surveillance. Most of these techniques, such as single entrances staffed by security or placement of windows and lines of sight to help increase observation of the premises, are difficult to address in homes, but even if they are present, defensible space theory proposes that neighbors plays an important role in maintaining the security of the neighborhood. According to this theory, transient home-sharing guests challenge this, because neighbors can no longer identify whether the presence of strangers is legitimate or not.

Rational choice theory suggests that would-be criminals rationally consider the costs and benefits of a bad act and choose to act if the benefits outweigh the costs. Crime in a hotel setting generally presents more costs to a criminal actor because there is a higher likelihood that they will be caught. In home sharing, costs are lower because home-sharing settings are decentralized and varied in terms of the implementation of security measures. Thus, according to this theory, home shares make for a more attractive location for crime on the part of both hosts and guests.

Routine activity theory predicts that crime is more likely when three things co-occur: (i) a motivated offender, (ii) a suitable target or victim, and (iii) in circumstances where the target lacks protection of a capable guardian. Under this theory, motivated offenders are assumed to be ever-present, and therefore, to prevent crime, the goal is to make a property appear less suitable a target and to provide a capable guardian. In that vein, hotels take steps to reduce the suitability of their buildings for crime by maintaining professional security and individualized locks on every hotel room door. Hotel guests likewise have some role as well to secure their valuables and be aware of their surroundings. Home-sharing hosts may take similar steps to hotels, but each home share will vary depending on the host. Similarly, home-sharing guests may be attentive to their security, but the extent to which that happens will vary as well. That said, hosts and guests themselves may present the biggest threat to each other. Home-sharing companies may provide education to both hosts and guests to reduce the event of problems, but there is no guarantee that users will pursue such tips.

In addition using these three theories to expose issues inherent in the home-sharing structure, the advent of the COVID-19 pandemic exposed additional problems. Hotels immediately adopted various approaches to cleaning and disinfecting their properties. Furthermore, they adopted friendly reimbursement policies for guests who needed to change their travel plans because of the virus. In contrast, the decentralized structure of home sharing made standardized cleaning difficult to achieve, because each host made their own decision on what to do. In addition, the refund process was very confusing, providing complaints on the part of both guests and hosts.

In the end, we see that the responsibility for safety and security lies on home-sharing users, but due to a lack of general understanding of this responsibility for various reasons, there has been a general reduction of safety and security for users and for the neighborhoods in which home sharing occurs. Home-sharing companies advise their users to implement their own safety and security measures, for example, on the VRBO website, users are advised to "always read over profiles and reviews" (VRBO 2020b), but studies have shown there is a lack of compliance with home-sharing companies' recommendations. For example, in 2015, when Zak Stone (2016), who lost his father to an accident in an Airbnb, researched this issue, he noted that 11,000 rentals in total were available to guests in Taiwan on Airbnb, and none of the hosts had to demonstrate working carbon monoxide detectors or permitting. Similarly, the National Fire Protection Association found a serious lack of compliance in installing fire alarms and smoke detectors (Kennedy et al. 2019, p. 328).

Airbnb emphasizes the trust between users is necessary for home sharing to be safe and secure, but others have stated that trust is insufficient (Lund-Durlacher et al. 2019). A member of the Westminster North UK parliament constituency defined the source of the problem as follows: "Residential neighbourhoods are turning into an extension of the hospitality industry without the necessary checks and support" (Ellery et al. 2018). Either "[t]here has to be more due diligence on the part of the … people that are renting out their properties" (McIntosh 2018), and a sense of shared responsibility needs to be embraced by all participating in the home-sharing sector (Mickle and Rana 2020) or new regulatory schemes need to be considered by policymakers.

8.1 Policy Recommendations

One preliminary step could be taken by the US Congress to address the liability shield for home-sharing companies. Section 230 of Communications and Decency Act (47 USC § 230) could be amended to carve out home sharing and make home-sharing companies more legally responsible for the risks that users undertake. Arguably, home sharing is substantively different than eBay, Etsy, and other Internet platforms that have been established to help users trade goods for money. In addition, home-sharing platforms are substantively different from social media platforms on which users share information, pictures, and videos. Home sharing places both hosts and guests in vulnerable places. This type of legislative change would make Airbnb and other home-sharing companies more responsible for experiences their users have. Companies would be incentivized to take steps to ensure hosts provide a safe and legal place to stay and guests behave in other people's homes.

Other possible policy amendments are suggested by the criminological theories explored in this research.

- Defensible space theory suggests that security would increase if home-sharing hosts were required to alert the neighborhood about the presence of their home share. A related policy could be to cap the number of home shares in a locality.

- Rational choice theory would encourage defining crimes related to home sharing in criminal law accompanied with significant levels of punishment, in the form of a fine or jail sentence, in order to alter the rational calculus of a potential bad actor.
- Routine activity theory suggests that reducing the number of potential crime victims in home sharing through a public outreach campaign that educates hosts and guests about how to protect themselves.

Further, the home-sharing sector can take lessons from practices developed by hotel management. In this sector, pre-employment drug tests and background checks are not required; yet, they are routinely performed by many of the larger hotel chains, with some of them screening all applicants whom they intend to hire (Krebs and Ricci 2004; Sommerville 2007). For others, this measure would be cost prohibitive (Krebs and Ricci 2004). For those that limit their screening to particular employees, experts recommend hotels conduct checks on employees who are responsible for large sums of money, such as bookkeepers, managers, and cashiers and employees who have high levels of customer contact, such as hotel bellhops, maids, room service wait staff, and delivery drivers (Sommerville 2007).

In home sharing, background checks are not routinely conducted on any users. Even though the Airbnb website states: "Globally we run hosts and guests against regulatory, terrorist and sanctions watchlists. For hosts and guests in the United States, we also conduct background checks" (Airbnb 2020b), another part of the website explains:

If we have enough information (usually the user's first and last name, plus date of birth) to identify a guest or host who lives in the United States, we check certain databases of public state and county criminal records, as well as state and national sex offender registries for criminal convictions and sex offender registrations (Airbnb 2020a).

In other words, background checks are not always done. Similarly, the VRBO website states: "We conduct certain background screening, where we're able to" (VRBO, "Trust and Safety"). This means the checks are not conducted on every user.

To improve safety and security, home-sharing companies could be required to do more extensive background checks on their users. Because hosts and guests enter into a fairly intimate relationship, each provides a significant risk to each other. While background checks can't prevent all crime, they can help to deter people with criminal histories from participating in home sharing for fear of being identified and provide a level of assurance to users.

Another practice hotels employ is to review photo identification from all hotel guests in person. This helps to ensure that the guests are who they say they are. It also ensures the hotel is aware of who is in their hotel rooms. In home sharing, this is not a standard practice. Airbnb states that hosts may do so, but it is neither mandatory nor are hosts instructed how to identify genuine IDs.

Under the current status, hosts and guests are responsible for their own safety and security and should take all necessary precautions. This is true especially when sharing homes are located in less touristy areas (Xu et al. 2017). The tips for both guests and hosts in Chap. 5, including understanding safety and security risks, methods to reduce those risks, and purchasing any necessary insurance, should be considered.

All these changes may make home sharing more safe and secure, but they may also make staying in a home share more expensive than it currently is. Studies like the one by Feickert et al. (2006) found hotel guests have high acceptance of security measures and some willingness to pay extra for them. It may be true that the same acceptance of a higher price point is worth the piece of mind.

8.2 Limitations and Future Research

This research, like all research, has some limitations, many of which present opportunities for more research. First and foremost, there is a dearth of crime and safety-related data, in terms of types of crimes and accidents as well as crime rates and accident rates for both hotels and home shares. There is no centralized collection of this information. Better insight and more nuanced conclusions could be had if these data were available. Further research should focus on collecting relevant data. Alternative sources of information, such as social media, including Reddit or Twitter, may be useful to analyze in this way. In addition, qualitative research based on interviews with hosts and guests would provide a deeper understanding of the risks and practices used by home-sharing users. Finally, the American Hotel and Lodging Association (ALHA) has claimed home sharing has been central to major crimes such as sex trafficking and terrorism. The ALHA is a biased source, considering the competition from home sharing to hotels. It will be important research to examine whether these crimes are occurring and how they could be prevented.

In addition, this research largely focused on Airbnb. Although Airbnb is the biggest home-sharing company in the market, an examination of other home-sharing companies would allow for analysis of varying policies and practices.

8.3 Conclusion

This research concludes by discussing the work of Lehr (2015) who reported on the changing competitive landscape in the hospitality industry with the entry of home-sharing companies like Airbnb. He found the "bright side" of shared accommodations to be "utopian" in nature, with the "dark side" resulting in increased housing costs and reduced inventory. He also discusses the absence of regulations on the part of home-sharing companies and the resulting mistreatment of homes by guests and misrepresentation of properties on the part of hosts. Lehr further reports the large increase of tourists in local areas and the large number of reportedly "illegal" Airbnb rental units at over 70%. As a result, he concludes residential areas are being operated commercially putting all parties at risk of violations. He also states the commercial safety standards are lacking when compared to hotels. In conclusion, he says "Caveat Emptor, 'let the buyer beware'" (pp. 2–3) Under the current circumstances, the authors agree.

Works Cited

Airbnb. (2020a). Does Airbnb perform background checks on its members? *Airbnb.com.* Retrieved from https://www.airbnb.com/help/article/1308/does-airbnb-perform-background-checks-on-members on June 28, 2020.

Airbnb. (2020b). Your safety is our priority. *Airbnb.com.* Retrieved from https://www.airbnb.com/trust on June 12, 2020.

Communications Decency Act of 1986, as amended in 1995, section 230 (47 USC § 230).

Ellery, B., Powell, M., & Atkinson, A. (2018). How Airbnb bandits rent out properties to prostitutes, drug dealers and party animals. *Dailymail.com,* December 30. Retrieved from https://www.dailymail.co.uk/news/article-6538881/How-Airbnb-bandits-rent-properties-prostitutes-drug-dealers-party-animals.html on July 4, 2020.

Feickert, J., Verma, R., Plaschka, G., & Dev, C. S. (2006). Safeguarding your customers. *Cornell Hotel and Restaurant Administration Quarterly, 47*(3), 224–244. https://doi.org/10.1177/0010880406288872.

Kennedy, H., et al. (2019). Reported fire safety and first-aid amenities in Airbnb venues in 16 American cities. *Injury Prevention, 25*, 328–330.

Krebs, R., & Ricci, P. (2004). Changing innkeepers' standard of care: Criminal background checks for prospective employees. *Electronic Journal of Hospitality, Legal, Safety and Security Research, II.*

Lehr, D. D. (2015). An analysis of the changing competitive landscape in the hotel industry regarding Airbnb. Dominican University of California Master's Thesis. Retrieved from https://scholar.dominican.edu/masters-theses/188/ from July 10, 2020.

Lund-Durlacher, D., Dinica, V., Reiser, D., & Fifka, M. S. (2019). *Corporate sustainability and responsibility in tourism.* Cham: Springer.

McIntosh, E. (2018). Airbnb rentals used for human trafficking, Toronto police say. *The Star.* Retrieved from https://www.thestar.com/news/crime/2018/02/22/airbnb-rentals-used-for-human-trafficking-toronto-police-say.html

Mickle, T., & Rana, P. (2020, April 28). 'A Bargain with the devil'-bill comes due for overextended Airbnb hosts. *Wall Street Journal,* April 28. Retrieved from https://www.wsj.com/articles/a-bargain-with-the-devilbill-comes-due-for-overextended-airbnb-hosts-11588083336 on July 10, 2020.

Sommerville, K. L. (2007). *Hospitality employee management and supervision: Concepts and practical applications.* Hoboken: Wiley.

Stone, Z. (2016). Living and dying on Airbnb. *Medium,* November 9. Retrieved from https://medium.com/matter/living-and-dying-on-airbnb-6bff8d600c04 on July 3, 2020.

VRBO. (2020a). Trust & safety. *VRBO.com.* Retrieved from https://www.vrbo.com/trust/traveler on June 28, 2020.

VRBO. (2020b). Terms and conditions. *VRBO.com.* Retrieved from https://www.vrbo.com/legal/terms-and-conditions on June 29, 2020.

Xu, Y. H., Kim, J. W., & Pennington-Gray, L. (2017). Explore the spatial relationship between Airbnb rental and crime. In *Proceedings from travel and tourism research association: Advancing tourism research globally.* Retrieved from https://scholarworks.umass.edu/cgi/viewcontent.cgi?article=2075andcontext=ttra on July 3, 2020.

Works Cited

Airbnb. (n.d.). Economic impact. *Airbnb.com*. Retrieved from https://blog.atairbnb.com/economic-impact-airbnb/ on April 15, 2020.

Airbnb. (2019). Recognizing the best in hospitality. *Airbnb.com*. Retrieved from https://www.airbnb.com/superhost on June 18, 2019.

Airbnb. (2020). How cancellations work for stays. *Airbnb.com*. Retrieved from https://www.airbnb.com/home/cancellation_policies on June 12, 2020.

American Hotel and Lodging Association. (n.d.). The U.S. hotel industry: Driving growth, jobs, and the economy. *American Hotel and Lodging Association*. Retrieved from https://www.ahla.com/sites/default/files/Driving%20Growth%2C%20Jobs%20and%20the%20Economy.pdf on July 10, 2020.

Bauman, A. (2019). Orinda shooting: Parents say Airbnb allowed dangerous party conditions that led to son's death. *San Francisco Chronicle*, November 8. Retrieved from https://www.sfchronicle.com/crime/article/Orinda-shooting-Parents-say-Airbnb-allowed-14818948.php on July 10, 2020.

Bauman, A., & Serrano, A. (2019). Orinda shooting: Following criticism, Airbnb says it will pay for funerals and counseling of victims. *San Francisco Chronicle*, November 8, Retrieved from https://www.sfchronicle.com/crime/article/Orinda-shooting-Airbnb-caves-to-criticism-and-14818638.php on July 10, 2020.

Bureau of Justice Statistics. (n.d.). *Crime characteristics and trends*. Retrieved from https://www.bjs.gov/index.cfm?ty=tpandtid=93 on July 2, 2020.

Cauley, J., & Im, E. (1988). Intervention policy analysis of skyjackings and other terrorist incidents. *American Economic Review, 78*(2), 27–31.

City of Oklahoma City. (n.d.). *Home sharing license*. Retrieved from https://www.okc.gov/departments/development-services/business-licensing/business-licenses/home-sharing-license on July 10, 2020.

City of Santa Monica Planning and Community Development. (2020). *Overview of the home-sharing ordinance*. Retrieved from https://www.smgov.net/Departments/PCD/Permits/Short-Term-Rental-Home-Share-Ordinance/ from July 10, 2020.

Clarke, R. V. G. (1980). 'Situational' crime prevention: Theory and practice. *The British Journal of Criminology, 20*(2), 136–147. https://doi.org/10.1093/oxfordjournals.bjc.a047153.

Cothren, J., Smith, B. L., Roberts, P., & Damphousse, K. R. (2008). Geospatial and temporal patterns of preparatory conduct among American terrorists. *International Journal of Comparative and Applied Criminal Justice, 32*(1), 23–41. https://doi.org/10.1080/01924036.2008.9678776.

C. A. Binns, R. J. Kempf, *Safety and Security in Hotels and Home Sharing*, SpringerBriefs in Criminology, https://doi.org/10.1007/978-3-030-59306-3

Cowley, J., Agro, C., & McDonald, J. (2019). 'I felt like a criminal': Airbnb hosts ask guests to lie, sneak around in covert rentals. *CBC News*, March 23. Retrieved from https://www.cbc.ca/news/business/marketplace-airbnb-covert-listings-banned-units-1.5066673 on July 10, 2020.

Cozens, P., & Love, T. (2017). The dark side of crime prevention through environmental design (CPTED). In *Oxford research encyclopedia of criminology and criminal justice*. https://doi.org/10.1093/acrefore/9780190264079.013.2.

Cozens, P., & Love, T. (2015). A review and current status of crime prevention through environmental design (CPTED). *Journal of Planning Literature, 30*(4), 393–412. https://doi.org/10.1177/0885412215595440.

Cozens, P. M., Saville, G., & Hillier, D. (2005). Crime prevention through environmental design (CPTED): A review and modern bibliography. *Property Management, 23*(5), 328–356. https://doi.org/10.1108/02637470510631483.

Crowe, T. D. (2000). *Crime prevention through environmental design: Applications of architectural design and space management concepts*. Boston: Butterworth-Heinemann.

Dorn, S. (2019). Boston tourist books Airbnb, gets rotting NYCHA apartment. *New York Post*, November 9. Retrieved from www.nypost.com/2019/11/09/boston-tourist-books-airbnb-gets-rotting-nycha-apartment/ on July 10, 2020.

Ekblom, P. (2010). Deconstructing CPTED... and reconstructing it for practice, knowledge management and research. *European Journal on Criminal Policy and Research, 17*(1), 7–28. https://doi.org/10.1007/s10610-010-9132-9.

Elster, J. (1986). *Rational choice*. New York: New York University Press.

Federal Emergency Management Agency. (2013). Defensible space and CPTED: Origins and applications. *FEMA.gov*. Retrieved from https://www.fema.gov/media-library-data/20130726-1624-20490-3298/430_a.pdf on July 10, 2020.

Grind, K., & Shifflett, S. (2019, December 26). *Shooting, sex crime and theft: Airbnb takes halting steps to protect its users*. https://www.wsj.com/articles/shooting-sex-crime-and-theft-airbnb-takes-halting-steps-to-police-its-platform-11577374845

Hale, C. (1996). Fear of crime: A review of the literature. *International Review of Victimology, 4*(2), 79–150. https://doi.org/10.1177/026975809600400201.

Hill, K. (2015). After a woman was poisoned in an Airbnb, the company started giving out prevention devices. *Splinter*, November 9. Retrieved from https://splinternews.com/after-a-woman-was-poisoned-in-an-airbnb-the-company-st-1793852717 on July 10, 2020.

Hilton. (2020). Hilton's commitment to you, our guests, as we navigate through coronavirus. *Hilton.com*, June 5. Retrieved from https://www.hilton.com/en/corporate/coronavirus/ on July 10, 2020.

Hsu, H. Y., & David, M. (2017). Does target-hardening result in deadlier terrorist attacks against protected targets? An examination of unintended harmful consequences. *Journal of Research in Crime and Delinquency, 54*(6), 930–957. https://doi.org/10.1177/0022427817719309.

Johns Hopkins Center for Injury Research and Policy, NYC Department of Health and Mental Hygiene, and Society for Public Health Education. (2013). *Active design supplement: Promoting safety*, Version 2.

Kettl, D. F. (2003). Contingent Coordination. *The American Review of Public Administration, 33*(3), 253–277. https://doi.org/10.1177/0275074003254472.

Keveney, B., & Oliver, D. (2020, April 02). What travelers, owners of Airbnb, Vrbo rentals should know about cancellations amid the coronavirus pandemic. *USA Today*, April 2. Retrieved from https://www.usatoday.com/story/travel/hotels/2020/04/02/coronavirus-what-travelers-hosts-airbnb-vrbo-rentals-should-know/5093115002/ on July 1, 2020.

Kiltz, L. (2011). The challenges of developing a homeland security discipline to meet future threats to the homeland. *Journal of Homeland Security and Emergency Management, 8*, 2. https://doi.org/10.2202/1547-7355.1899.

Lock, S. (2019). Hotel industry – Statistics & facts. *Statista.com*, June 18. Retrieved from www.statista.com/topics/1102/hotels/ on July 10, 2020.

Love, T. (2016). *Airbnb's revenue soars 89 percent. San Francisco Business Times*, September 1. Retrieved from https://www.bizjournals.com/sanfrancisco/news/2016/09/01/airbnbs-revenue-soars-compared-to-hotels.html on July 10, 2020.

Marriott Bonvoy. (2020). Travel information COVID-19 update. *Marriott.com*, July 6. Retrieved from https://marriott-re-2019ncovc.com/?ES=SM_TWTR_3217717971 on July 10, 2020.

Marsh, J. (2016). AirBnb renter duped into paying $9K for dingy apartment: Suit. *New York Post*, August 30. Retrieved from https://nypost.com/2016/08/30/airbnb-renter-duped-into-paying-9k-for-dingy-apartment-suit/ on July 10, 2020.

Matijosaitiene, I., & Petriashvili, A. (2017). Urban planning and design for terrorism resilient cities. *Journal of Sustainable Architecture and Civil Engineering, 18*(1), 27–38. https://doi.org/10.5755/j01.sace.18.1.15443.

Matusitz, J. A. (2015). *Symbolism in terrorism: Motivation, communication, and behavior*. Lanham: Rowman and Littlefield.

McGee, J. (2001). Ex-FBI officials criticize tactics on terrorism. *The Washington Post*, November 28. Retrieved from www.washingtonpost.com/archive/politics/2001/11/28/ex-fbi-officials-criticize-tactics-on-terrorism/51b59615-12bd-4c72-97dc-859183d12640/?noredirect=on on July 10, 2020.

Meyjes, T. (2019). Paedophile 'advertised Harry Potter-inspired cupboard for £10 a night on Airbnb'. *Metro.co.uk*, December 12. Retrieved from https://metro.co.uk/2017/05/14/paedophile-advertised-harry-potter-inspired-cupboard-for-10-a-night-on-airbnb-6636121/ on July 10, 2020.

Moffatt, I. (1983). Modelling the environment as a dynamic system. *Environmental Conservation, 10*(4), 348–349. https://doi.org/10.1017/s0376892900013084.

Molla, R. (2017). Airbnb is on track to rack up more than 100 million stays this year - and that's only the beginning of its threat to the hotel industry. *Vox*, July 19. Retrieved from https://www.vox.com/2017/7/19/15949782/airbnb-100-million-stays-2017-threat-business-hotel-industry on July 10, 2020.

Mzezewa, T. (2019). Airbnb and Miami Beach are at war. Travelers are caught in the crossfire. *The New York Times*, March 9. Retrieved from www.nytimes.com/2019/03/09/travel/airbnb-miami-beach-war.html on July 10, 2020.

National Crime Prevention Council. (2009). Best practices for using crime prevention through environmental design in weed and seed sites. Retrieved from https://www.ncpc.org/wp-content/uploads/2017/11/NCPC_BestPracticesCPTED.pdf on July 10, 2020.

National Crime Prevention Council. (2020). Crime prevention through environmental design. *NCPC.org*. Retrieved from www.ncpc.org/resources/home-neighborhood-safety/crime-prevention-through-environmental-design-training-program/ on July 10, 2020.

New Jersey Safe Routes to School Resource Center and Edward J. Bloustein School of Planning and Public Policy, Rutgers, The State University of New Jersey. (2017). *Employing crime prevention through environmental design in the NJ safe routes to school program: A review of literature and recommendations*. Retrieved from http://www.saferoutesnj.org/wp-content/uploads/2018/09/SRTS-CPTED-Topic-Report.pdf on July 10, 2020.

Newman, O. (1996). *Creating defensible space*. Diane Publishing.

Marketwired. (2013). New study: Airbnb generated $632 million in economic activity in New York. Marketwired. *Yahoo Finance*, October 22. Retrieved from https://finance.yahoo.com/news/study-airbnb-generated-632-million-162140758.html on July 10, 2020.

Nunn, S. (2005). Preventing the next terrorist attack: The theory and practice of homeland security information systems. *Journal of Homeland Security and Emergency Management, 2*(3), 1–28. https://doi.org/10.2202/1547-7355.1137.

Oliveira, N. (2020). Florida orders all visitors from NYC area to self-quarantine for 2 weeks. *New York Daily News*, March 24. Retrieved from https://www.nydailynews.com/coronavirus/ny-coronavirus-florida-orders-nyc-area-visitors-to-self-quarantine-20200324-6knewexnd-bap7hqjruyoyflsgu-story.html on July 10, 2020.

Ostrom, E. (1998). A behavioral approach to the rational choice theory of collective action: Presidential address, American political science association, 1997. *American Political Science Review, 92*(1), 1–22. https://doi.org/10.2307/2585925.

Reynald, D. M. (2010). Translating CPTED into crime preventive action: A critical examination of CPTED as a tool for active guardianship. *European Journal on Criminal Policy and Research, 17*(1), 69–81. https://doi.org/10.1007/s10610-010-9135-6.

Rodriguez, S. (2020). Airbnb feels the crunch as governments ban short-term rentals. *CNBC*, April 17. Retrieved from https://www.cnbc.com/2020/04/16/airbnb-hosts-feel-the-crunch-of-coronavirus-short-term-rental-bans.html on July 10, 2020.

Saville, G., & Cleveland, G. (2008). Second-generation CPTED. *21st Century Security and CPTED* (pp. 79–90). https://doi.org/10.1201/9781420068085.ch7.

Silberman, C. E. (1980). *Criminal violence, criminal justice*. New York: Random House.

Sommerville, K. L. (2007). *Hospitality employee management and supervision: Concepts and practical applications*. Hoboken: Wiley.

Staff Author. (2020). Leading Hotel Companies. *Investopedia*, May 12. Retrieved from www.investopedia.com/articles/investing/061015/top-5-most-profitable-hotel-companies.asp on July 10, 2020.

Stark, R. (1987). Deviant places: A theory of the ecology of crime. *Criminology, 25*(4), 893–910. https://doi.org/10.1111/j.1745-9125.1987.tb00824.x.

Stoller, G. (2013). Hotel guests face carbon monoxide risk. *USA Today*, January 9. Retrieved from https://www.usatoday.com/story/travel/hotels/2012/11/15/hotels-carbon-monoxide/1707789/ on July 10, 2020.

St. Petersburg Police Department. (n.d.). *CPTED Brochure*. Retrieved from https://police.stpete.org/crime-prevention/brochures/cpted-brochure.pdf on March 15, 2020.

Trejos, N. (2013). Hotels set aside floors for women. *USA Today*, December 9. Retrieved from https://www.usatoday.com/story/travel/hotels/2013/12/08/hotels-women-only-floors/3910931/ on July 10, 2020.

United States Department of Homeland Security. (n.d.). Target hardening: Prevention through environmental design. Resource guide. Retrieved from https://www.hsdl.org/?view&did=765806 on July 10, 2020.

Yancey, W. L. (1971). Architecture, interaction, and social control. *Environment and Behavior, 3*(1), 3–21. https://doi.org/10.1177/001391657100300101.

Index

A
Academic theories, 59
Accidental death, 15
Accidents, 83–85, 88
Airbnb
  accident, 86
  bookings, 78
  cleaning and disinfecting
    process, 78
  communication and payment, 84
  and crime, 16
  economic impact, 2
  extenuating circumstance policy, 79
  guest's safety and security, 34
  and hacking, 47
  heterogeneous effects, 16
  home sharing listings, 38
  home-sharing company, 1
  hosts, 6
  international destinations
    in 2019, 12
  market share, 2
  nightmare, 51
  primary markets, 2
  primary safety/security feature, 55
  properties, 12, 19, 22
  refunds and rescheduling, 78
  rental, 2
  revenue, 13
  risks of COVID-19, 78
  safety risks, 78
  smoke detectors, 7
  superhost, 35
  verified identification, 35
  and VRBO, 2, 3
  website, 47
Airbnb activity, 16
Airbnb's rule, 53
The American Hotel and Lodging Association
    (ALHA), 88
American Red Cross (ARC), 23
Anecdotal evidence, 16, 23
Assault, 18

B
Background checks, 47
Bait and switch, 19, 21
Biggest hotel providers, 11, 12
Brothels, 21

C
Cancelation policies, 79
Child sex assault, 18
Cleaning protocols, 78
Cleaning standards, 78
Closed-circuit television
    (CCTV), 32
Comparative analysis, 44
Coronavirus, 77
  See also COVID-19
Cost, 83, 85, 87, 88
Cost-benefit analysis, 52

C. A. Binns, R. J. Kempf, *Safety and Security in Hotels and Home Sharing*, SpringerBriefs in Criminology, https://doi.org/10.1007/978-3-030-59306-3

COVID-19, 1, 5
advent, 77, 80
extenuating circumstance, 79
outbreak, 77
pandemic, 13
safety risks, 78
self-quarantine, 79
Crime analysis, 16
Crime prevention, 60, 68
Crime triangle, 68
Crimes, 83–85, 87, 88
fake listings, 17
home-sharing setting, 17
illegal listings, 17
Criminals
criminal activity, 68
potential offenders, 70
rational choice theory, 65
rational criminal actor, 66
rational decision makers, 65
terrorist's motivation, 66
theories, 71
Criminological theories, 65, 71

D
Defensible space theory, 59–62, 64, 85, 86
Discrimination, 18
Drug manufacturing, 18
Drug use, 18

E
Extenuating circumstance policy, 79

F
Fake listings, 17, 18, 21, 23
Federal Communications Decency Act of 1986, section 230, 33
Federal Hotel and Motel Fire Safety Act of 1989, 31
Federal Trade Commission (FTC), 33
Fire safety, 31
Frauds, 19, 20
Full cash refund, 79, 80

G
Gig economy, 11
Guests, 4

H
Hacking, 18
Hand sanitizer, 78
Harassment, 18, 20
Hilton Worldwide Holdings, 11
Home shares
cost, 83
crimes, 17, 18
data, 17
guests' safety and security concerns, 44
in jurisdiction, 84
laws (*see* Laws on safety and security)
safety and security, 83
safety concerns, 83
Home sharing, 19, 53
Airbnb, 12 (*see also* Airbnb)
companies, 2
COVID-19 pandemic, 85
defensible space theory, 62, 64
future research, 88
gig economy, 11
guests, 85
hospitality, 83
hosts, 3, 4, 6
legal landscape, 5
meteoric rise, 12
online review systems, 21
providers, 1
regulation, 84
revenue, 63
routine activity theory, 70
safe and secure, 86
safety concerns, 3
safety measures, 3
security concerns, 3, 16
security measures, 3
settings, 85
sites, 11
standardized cleaning, 85
through Internet, 12
users, 4, 85
VRBO, 2
Home-sharing companies, 3, 39
crimes and accidents, 83
home-sharing platforms, 86
hosts, 83
legal matter, 84
market, 88
recommendations, 84
transaction, 84
VRBO website, 86
Home-sharing sector, 6
Home-sharing services, 5

Hospitality, 83, 84, 86, 88
Hospitality industry, 11, 13
Host's property, 18
Hotel guests, 53, 85, 87, 88
Hotel's obligation
 fire safety, 31
 to guests' personal money and baggage, 31
 to guests' personal safety and security, 30, 31
 terrorism, 32
Hotel-guest relationship, 32
Hotels
 companies, 12
 competition, 2
 defensible space concept, 62
 description, 3
 fire/gas leak, 30
 full-time business, hospitality, 1
 funds, 21
 illegal activity, 30
 innkeeper laws (*see* Innkeeper laws)
 inspection, 7
 legal and regulatory responsibilities, 31
 legal landscape, 5
 legal remedies, 32
 lodging, 3
 nonpayment, 32
 public accommodations, 11
 routine activity theory, 69
 security guards, 67
 types, 3
 U.S., 1

I
Illegal brothels, 22
Illegal listings, 17, 18, 21, 22
Illegal videotaping, 18
Initial public offering (IPO), 13
Innkeeper laws
 early English common law, 29
 guest's property, 31
 innkeeper's control, 30
 landlords and tenants, 40
 legal duty, 29
 legal expectations, 29
 on peer relationships, 39
 safety and security, 29
 traditional role, 30
Insurance companies, 39
InterContinental Hotel Group, 11
Internet platform companies, 33

K
Kidnapping, 18

L
Landlords, 38
Landlord-tenant law, 39
Laws on safety and security
 Communications and Decency Act, 33
 Federal Communications Decency Act of 1986, section 230, 33
 FTC, 33
 Gentry v. eBay, Inc., 33–34
 Internet platform companies, 33
Legal liability
 in hotels and home shares, 29, 30
Legal obligations, 44, 49, 52
Limitations, 88

M
Mandatory regulations, 84
Marriott International, 2, 11
Media analysis, 16
Motor vehicle theft, 16
Multiple Dwelling Law, 36–38
Multiresident buildings, 61
Murder, 15, 18

N
National crime victimization survey (NCVS), 16, 17
National Fire Protection Association, 86
Neighborhood watch program, 61
Newman's theory, 60
New York home-sharing regulation, 35, 36, 39

P
Pandemic, 77, 78
 See also COVID-19
Pedophile host, 18
Pervasive, 21
Phony listings, 19
Policy recommendations
 background checks, 87
 criminal convictions, 87
 defensible space theory, 86
 home sharing, 86
 hosts and guests, 87
 photo identification, 87
 policy amendments, 86

Policy recommendations (*cont.*)
- pre-employment drug tests, 87
- rational choice theory, 87
- routine activity theory, 87
- VRBO, 87

Private causes of action, 39
Private dwellings, 36
Property crime, 16
Property-related scams, 20
Property victimizations, 17
Prostitution, 18

Q

Qualitative research, 88
Quarantine, 77, 79
Quarantine orders, 79

R

Rape, 18
Rational choice theory, 65–68, 85, 87
Recommendations, 59
Refunds, 78
Rescheduling, 78
Responsibility
- companies, 6
- for crime control and prevention, 4
- home sharing, 5, 6
- on hotels, 83
- for safety and security, 4–6

Revenue, 12, 13
Routine activity theory, 68–70, 85, 87

S

Safety and security concerns, 43–46, 49, 63
Safety and security practices, 44–46, 50–52, 55, 56
Safety concerns, 3
- deficiencies, 23
- free smoke and carbon monoxide detectors, 23
- in hotels and home shares, 23

Safety measures, 3
Safety tips
- for guests and hosts, 48
- for home-sharing guests, 54, 55
- for home-sharing hosts, 55

Sanitization techniques, 78
SARs-CoV-2, 77
- *See also* COVID-19

Security
- agents, 61
- and administrative staff, 69
- defensible space, 59, 62
- design prototype, 60
- experts, 71
- patrols, 71
- rational choice theory, 65
- visible security alarms, 67
- vulnerabilities, 59

Security concerns, 3
- in hotels and home shares, 17
- NCVS, 17

Security measures, 3
Security models, 5–6
Security outcomes, 6
Security systems, 32
Self-quarantine, 79
Sex trafficking, 88
Sexual harassment, 18
Situational crime prevention, 68, 71
Smoke/carbon monoxide detectors, 7
Special travel insurance, 39
Squatting, 18
Standard of care, 30
Strict cancelation policy, 79
Superhosts, 34, 35

T

Target hardening, 65, 67, 69, 71
Terrorism, 32, 88
Theft, 18
Tourism services, 1
Travel bans, 79
Travel services, 1

V

Vandalism, 18
Verified identification, 35
Violation, 18, 21

W

Wyndham Worldwide, 2

Z

Zero obligation, 52

The manufacturer's authorised representative in the EU is Springer Nature Customer Service Centre GmbH, Europaplatz 3, 69115 Heidelberg, Germany. If you have any concerns regarding our products, please contact ProductSafety@springernature.com

Printed and bound by CPI Group (UK) Ltd, Croydon, CR0 4YY
01/10/2026
02226351-0011